The Ripple Eclipse

turning the tide of inherited trauma

Audrey Hyams Romoff

ISBN 978-1-998206-49-0 (paperback)

ISBN 978-1-998206-50-6 (e-book)

First Edition

Published by RE:BOOKS Publishing

www.rebooks.ca

Back Cover Credits:

Photographer: David Hawe david@davidhawe.com

Makeup: Dino Dilio, info@dinodilio.com

Hair: Lani Starr, hairbylanistarr@gmail.com

Design: Chloe Faith Robinson

Author Picture Credits:

Photographer: David Hawe, david@davidhawe.com

Makeup: Dino Dilio, info@dinodilio.com

Hair: Hair By Toula

Cover Design by Chelsea Brooks Smith

Interior Design by Chloe Faith Robinson

Praise for *The Ripple Eclipse*

"This is not a tale of tidy healing, but a fearless excavation of what it means to live, grieve, and keep moving forward. Hyams Romoff writes with the precision of a publicist and the vulnerability of a survivor—each page both polished and painfully true. The result is a memoir that burns with honesty, but glimmers with hope."

—CANREADS Book Review

"Startlingly compelling . . . a powerful and emotional work."

—Kirkus Book Review

"Brave, pure, and unflinching, *The Ripple Eclipse,* is a rare love letter to the secrets we all bury within. Where generational pain is not hidden—but honoured, understood, and transformed. Audrey Hyams Romoff offers an invitation to confront the past with compassion and humour by providing a map towards self-discovery and liberation. A necessary read for anyone carrying the weight of what came before."

—Amanda Brugel, actor

"A deeply honest and reflective memoir, this book explores the intergenerational transmission of trauma. The author examines the painful legacy of her family's Holocaust survival and the invisible wounds that shaped her upbringing. As she navigates her healing journey, she faces the enduring impact of the past with courage and resilience, ultimately fostering hope for herself and for future generations."

—Simone Levey, Ph.D., C. Psych, Co-Founder of RENNI

"An honest look at generational trauma and monumental grief. Eloquently written and full of heart, it details her experiences moving through more loss than one person should ever have to bear. Audrey's words are introspective, but she manages to weave in enough humour to walk us through her most painful memories, making this a deeply personal and beautiful memoir. I think the world needs this book more than it knows. I am a more compassionate person for having read it and will be encouraging everyone I know to do the same."

—Sara Waisglass, actor

This book is dedicated to:

Mom, even imperfect love is still love.

Dad, the cost of unconditional love is the shadow of unconditional pain.

My resilient, spectacular grandmother.

Michael, for sharing the journey together, in the sunshine and the storms.

Lindsay and Alex, a love that knows no bounds. I am so proud to be your mother.

Rachel and Brahm Hyams.

Dear Mummy,

Have a marvelous Mother's Day, you are a great Mom,

the best, and I'll try and be a good kid.

P.S. I Love You

— Audrey, Mother's Day card, age 8

"It seems to me that there is something that tells us to tell our story to leave some kind of an imprint."

—Rachel, August 15, 1994, interview transcript from *Kinderlager* (Milton J. Nieuwsma)

My grandmother, my mother, my daughter, and me.
Four generations of women strapped into the front car of a
House of Horrors amusement park ride.
Behind each sharp bend, a new trauma, ready to jump out at us:
Violent death; suicide; drugs; and alcohol.
Each of us inadvertently leaking grief for the others to absorb.

Gone

My parents, Rachel and Brahm, were missing. I last saw them seven hours earlier, on the back porch of the beautiful red-brick house where I grew up in Montreal. It was Wednesday, October 1, 2008. A sunny, unseasonably warm day. My husband Michael and I, along with our children, Lindsay, sixteen, and Alex, fourteen, had stopped by the house to say goodbye before driving back home to Toronto. Our last stop at the end of a quick two-day family visit.

It was the morning of the second day of Rosh Hashanah—the Jewish New Year, the beginning of the High Holiday season. Michael and I had been doing these trips for twenty-five years since I'd moved to Toronto. A meticulously orchestrated schedule designed to ensure that each of our families got equal time. Dinner with Michael's family, dinner with my family, attending synagogue, seeing friends.

My mother was wearing her bright yellow matching sweatshirt and sweatpants (the signature leisure outfit behind her self-appointed nickname of Nana Banana). I still couldn't wrap my head around how my fashion-obsessed mother, at seventy-one, now often looked like she was wearing adult Garanimal outfits, the mix-and-match separates brand from my childhood.

Lindsay said goodbye, then Alex, then Michael, until it was just me standing in the doorway with my parents. "I'm going straight to work when I get back, so don't worry if I forget to call you," I said. My mother was a worrier. Calling upon arrival was a mandatory ritual to ensure that no harm befell us en route.

My father turned to my mother. "See, Rachel?" he said. "Audrey's going to call you when she gets home." I noted it because it seemed so out of context.

There was no lingering embrace. We were not a family of huggers. I climbed into the passenger seat of our Mercedes SUV. As Michael drove away, I turned back and waved.

Six hours later in Toronto, we made a quick pit stop at the house for Michael and the kids to disembark, and then I drove to the office. The PR agency I own leased the top two floors of a heritage-designated house that had been converted into office space. Michael bought the property years earlier. There was a fire escape off my office, which was excellent for smoking and watching baby raccoons climb the balcony next door. My parents didn't know I smoked. My father was a radiologist and read X-rays for lung cancer all the time. He would have been furious with me.

I called my parents at 5 p.m. that day to tell them that we had indeed arrived home safely. No answer. Their ancient answering machine—with my mother politely asking the caller to leave a message—didn't pick up.

Odd.

I was working on a big event for a major magazine publishing company. Anthony Zuiker, the creator of the CSI franchise, was the special guest. My agency's job was to transform a huge event space into a crime-scene-themed party. There was still so much to do: check the guest list, finalize the décor, make sure everything ran perfectly. I kept working and, in between tasks, calling my parents and smoking a cigarette on the fire escape. Then calling again. Every fifteen minutes.

No answer.

ODD.

I called Michael and told him I was worried. "They've probably gone for a walk," he said.

Smoke. Work. Call. Repeat. For hours.

VERY, VERY ODD.

The second time I called Michael, he said, "Maybe the phone service is down." It felt like a stretch. After several hours of working and calling, I left the office at midnight.

I went home and painted my long fingernails blood red. I don't know why. In my anxious state, it just somehow seemed appropriate. I went to bed at 1 a.m. with my cell phone next to my head.

At 6:30 a.m., I started calling my parents again. My father is an early riser. Nothing. It was now almost twenty-four hours since I'd last spoken with them. At 7:30 a.m., I had my father paged at the hospital. He didn't answer. I had another doctor in his department paged. No response.

By this point, I was convinced that something terrible must have happened. There was no other reasonable explanation.

My mundane daily routine took over, and I kept moving ahead, as if it were just a regular day. I pretended I wasn't encased in fear . . . that I could focus on other things. The kids got ready for school. Michael drove off with Alex.

I had an event later that day so had to keep moving. I was going to take Lindsay to school, then visit my stylist for my tri-weekly blowout.

I took a bath. Normal . . . just act normal. I climbed into the hot water and stared at the ceiling. Once I got out of the bath, I wrapped myself in a towel. I should have been deciding what to wear, but instead, I called Michael again. I started telling him that I still couldn't reach my parents. "Audrey, they're gone," he said. I didn't understand. Gone? Gone where? And then he said, "They're dead."

It was the milkman who discovered them early in the morning on October 2. Yes, we still had milk delivery service in Montreal in 2008. He had to walk by the detached double-car garage to get to the back door, where he always dropped their delivery off. As he did, he noticed, through a window, that the light was on in the garage. The garage door was closed. He looked in and saw them. My parents. He called 911, but it was too late.

With that phone call, everything was blown to smithereens. A steel door slamming shut, bisecting my life into Before and After.

I made a promise to myself that day. This legacy stops here. No more secrets. Secrets kill. This was what I call the Ripple Eclipse. The tiny waves that emanated from my mother, the same waves that now threatened to block out all the light.

How the fuck was I going to fight my way out of this darkness?

BEFORE

Rutka and Regina

MY MOTHER WAS BORN RUTKA GREENSPAN in Tomaszów Mazowiecki, Poland, in 1937. Following multiple name changes and marriage, she became Rachel Hyams. She was the first and ultimately only child of my grandparents, Regina and Aaron Greenspan.

The Greenspans were a young married couple who had every reason to believe they had a bright, beautiful future. They both came from large families.

My grandmother had three siblings. Mania, her eldest sister, had blue eyes, striking blonde hair, and was the town beauty. My grandmother had chestnut-coloured hair and beautiful dark eyes. Itzhak, her brother, introduced my grandparents to one another. He was the best man at their wedding in 1935. Sarah, the youngest, was also married.

Tomaszów had a large Jewish community. Its founder had invited Jewish entrepreneurs to settle there in the early 1820s, and the Jewish community was officially recognized by 1831.

Construction of the Great Synagogue began in 1846. By the early 1900s, its Jewish residents made up nearly half of the city's population. The people of the town suffered greatly under German occupation during the First World War, but after Poland's independence in 1918, life significantly improved in the region. In the 1930s, several Jewish political parties were active, and the community was thriving.

The Greenspans had a wonderful existence in Tomaszów. Aaron ran a successful transportation business. Family and friends gathered for weddings, birthdays, and Jewish holidays. But in 1939, the prosperity that my grandparents and their families had come to know evaporated. Tomaszów was one of the first areas of Poland that fell to Nazi occupation. My mother was two years old. By 1940, the Jewish population was moved into ghettos. The following year, the ghettos were sealed off from the outside world.

My mother's earliest childhood memory was of hiding in a cellar with other people. She assumes it was soon after the ghetto was established. My grandmother was scared because her husband wasn't with them, and she didn't know where he was. This became a pattern. My grandfather disappearing and reappearing. Regina and Rutka always together.

What my mother remembered about her father was that he was very passionate about her and that, in his eyes, she could do no wrong. If Regina tried to discipline her, he would always intervene on her behalf. He was very handsome too, always throwing her in the air and smothering her with kisses.

By November 2, 1942, winter had set in. A white frost blanketed the ghetto, the bombed-out buildings, and the remains of the Great Synagogue, destroyed by the German occupiers in 1939. Three days earlier, the Nazis began removing people from their homes, street by street, with the aim of entirely emptying the ghetto. At dawn, the Gestapo soldiers began their rounds. My mother was only five years old, but she said she remembered that morning. The herding. Men and women, the elderly and children, all lined up in rows on the streets. The Gestapo banging on doors and shouting, *"Alle Juden raus!"* All Jews outside. It was repeated in Yiddish and Polish for the many who did not speak German.

I don't know if she saw the slow and the sick being shot down in the streets by machine guns. If she heard the children screaming as they were separated from their parents—those parents knowing they would likely never see their children again. The ghetto's inhabitants had been living this Groundhog Day nightmare for nearly three years, and now, the horror was escalating.

My mother and grandmother were in a group that was directed toward a small church on Wajtsznosc Street. In the courtyard, the Gestapo inspected the work permits of the Jewish residents and decided who would remain in the ghetto and who would be deported. People were separated into different lines. There were always different lines. At some point, my mother's grandparents vanished.

If you were put in the line by the gate of the churchyard, you survived, at least on that day. If you were sent to the other line, you were herded into cattle cars destined for the forced labour and extermination camps in Treblinka (where over 700,000 Jews were killed in just sixteen months). Of course, my mother could not have known these details, but she must have absorbed the panic and terror all around her. Records show that in those three days, approximately 15,000 people from Tomaszów were deported to Treblinka. Regina, Aaron, and Rutka were among the several hundred people left behind. Many of their family members, gone.

Soldiers directed my mother and grandmother to a corner of the ghetto where several large stacks sat like piles of raked leaves.

I imagine that, at first, they couldn't make out the details of these strange masses. But as they got closer, the contents of each pile grew more defined. They were looking at the personal belongings of friends, neighbours, family. People who would no longer need their things. Eyeglasses. Shoes. Shirts. Stockings. Their job was to sort through the jumbled remains of other people's lives, looking for items of value for the Nazis.

They remained in what my grandmother Regina called "the little ghetto" for six months until the spring of 1943, when they, along with the other inhabitants of the ghetto, were sent to the Starachowice labour camp, 70 miles southeast. After this, there were no Jews left in Tomaszów.

My grandmother was put to work in a munitions factory. Young children didn't accompany their parents but, for some reason, even though my mother was only six years old, she was allowed to go with my grandmother.

Not long after their arrival, they began to witness another round of selections. Trucks appeared every few days to gather up those who were sick or not meeting their work quotas. None of the people who were pulled out ever returned. It was a death sentence.

By now, these imprisoned Jews had begun to take a more proactive approach to their survival. If you were able to bribe an SS guard, you would be given a warning about the roundups. Aaron did what he could to protect his family. These bribes provided him with advance notice, and a safe place for his wife and child to hide during the selections. When the signal came, they stole away into a specific corner of an attic as instructed. There were usually several other people there with them. My mother most clearly remembered an elderly Hasidic Jew lying face down on the floor and praying.

The soldiers arrived, sticking their bayonets through the cracks in the wooden ceiling. Then the shooting began. The little group remained safe in their designated corner despite someone tipping off the Nazis about their hiding place. The Nazis avoided targeting that corner. The soldiers knew exactly where they were hiding. The bribe was successful.

In the summer of 1944, news trickled down that Starachowice was being cleared out. My grandparents considered their options . . . die now, or face almost certain death in a concentration camp. My seven-year-old mother overheard her parents discussing suicide. Aaron had acquired access to a lethal drug. My pragmatic grandmother then asked her husband, "But who will give the poison to Rutka?" It would have to happen in that order. My mother first. Neither of them could bring themselves to end their child's life. At least they were all together. For now.

By the time Starachowice closed, only a handful of Jewish children from Tomaszów had survived. This included my mother, five-year-old Tova Friedman, and ten-year-old Frieda Grayzel. Many years later, all three were profiled in the book *Kinderlager,* by Milton Nieuwsma.

My mother distinctly remembered getting on the train car with my grandmother on the morning they were shipped out of Starachowice. They were bound for Auschwitz. The men were put on a different train to Dachau.

From inside that overcrowded train car waiting to begin their terrible journey, my mother saw a young man standing outside the train. He was wearing a navy-blue pea coat but was completely naked below the waist. She had been aware of someone mentally ill in the camp and assumed it was him. He was not put on the train with the other men. When the train pulled away, he was just left there. Alone. For some reason, I can't get that image out of my mind. A little girl, packed into a train car, peeking out at this strange young man who was left behind to die.

The train pulled away. My mother never saw her father again.

My grandmother was told that her husband had suffocated in the cattle car. She was a widow at twenty-four. She did not tell my mother that her father was dead until after the war ended, offering a vague explanation that he didn't make it off the train alive.

When Regina and Rutka arrived in Auschwitz, they were still in fairly good health. It was June of 1944. My mother remembered being in some sort of large building. They had no possessions and were given clothes to change in to. Surprisingly, they did not have their heads shorn or receive number tattoos at that time. My mother later speculated that the Nazis, who were efficiency experts, didn't want to waste their resources carrying out those activities on a mother and young child not considered valuable in the concentration camp ecosystem. My grandmother vividly recalled them being marched in front of Dr. Josef Mengele, the SS physician nicknamed the "Angel of Death" for the deadly and inhumane experiments he carried out at Auschwitz.

My mother eventually did receive a tattoo in August 1944: A-27632. She said she remembered that it hurt, and that her arm swelled, the number raised on the inflamed skin.

There was definitely an element of luck to their survival with the Nazi infrastructure collapsing as the Russian front advanced—but there was more to it than that. A fierce group of resourceful mothers who banded together to try to save their children.

The children's food rations consisted only of bread. Sometimes it was coarse, and other times, resembled soft white sandwich bread. One of the kapos (the name for a prisoner appointed by the

SS as a supervisor) gave my mother extra rations because she said she resembled her favourite niece.

If a child got ill and could not eat the coarse bread, my grandmother would give them my mother's soft bread. Even in that situation, where the Nazis were doing everything in their power to dehumanize and degrade them, Regina maintained her humanity and was able to share small acts of kindness.

After they were liberated, Regina and Rutka tried to find the kapo to thank her, but she had vanished.

My mother said she didn't feel scared at first. She felt protected by her mother and the other adults there. In her mind, this was what made all the difference. No matter what horrors were taking place around her, she was living inside a small protective bubble.

And then that changed. All the children were ordered to move to the Kinderlager, a barracks established by Dr. Mengele to give him unfettered access to subjects for his experiments. When they came to take my mother, Regina started screaming. When my mother looked back as she was being dragged away, she saw my grandmother being clubbed over the head by SS guards. She later described it as feeling like her mother had disappeared.

They were now separated by an electrified fence. Whenever possible, my grandmother would try to get extra food rations from the kitchen. Sometimes they would beat her, but other times they would give her something. She tried to throw food parcels over the fence to her daughter, but it was too far away, and the parcels always landed in the space between the fences.

There are episodes my mother remembered that will never be explained. One day, the SS guards came into the Kinderlager and moved all the children to a different building, telling them to undress. The building they were moved to was one of the gas chambers and crematoriums. And then, nothing happened. The children were taken back to the Kinderlager.

My mother slept in an upper bunk with a red blanket that resembled a shag carpet. There was a brick oven down the middle of the barracks that provided heat. She told me she was never cold, beaten, or abused there. She just missed her mother.

After they were separated, my grandmother either feigned illness or was genuinely sick, and was moved to the hospital barracks, which was close to the Kinderlager. There, they were no longer separated by an electrified fence.

In January of 1945, an order came down that Auschwitz was to be evacuated.

It was cold, and my mother and grandmother had no warm clothing or shoes. Their health had significantly deteriorated over the last six months. Regina then made a decision that likely saved their lives. She knew there was no way that they would survive if they evacuated with the others. In her mind, if this was the end and they were going to die anyway, then they may as well stay in the camp. They hid in the lower part of a bunk bed and covered themselves with piles of filthy blankets. My mother told me that she could sense my grandmother was in a different place in terms of her own resources and her capability to survive. She was resigned to their fate.

Most of the prisoners evacuated the camp on January 17, 1945, in what history books now refer to as "The Death March from Auschwitz." Sixty thousand prisoners were evacuated. Fifteen thousand of them died on the days-long marches.

Regina and Rutka were among the six thousand prisoners who survived by staying and hiding. The camp was totally silent. After ten days, they heard shouting from afar. The hidden prisoners assumed the Nazis had returned. There was panic and tears. This was finally goodbye. There was nothing else to be done. They anticipated the worst.

The shouting was, in fact, the approaching Russian army. On January 27, 1945, my mother saw what she referred to as "apparitions" enter the camp. They spoke Russian and were followed by mobile army soup kitchens.

It had been six years since the creation of the Tomaszów ghetto. My mother and grandmother had survived but were not the same. The vivacious, curious two-year-old was now an emaciated eight-year-old. Regina was a widow. Her entire family perished. They had been "liberated," but what does liberation mean when you have nothing to go back to and nowhere to go?

They remained in Auschwitz until July of that year, when Noah Greenspan, one of my grandfather's younger brothers, magically appeared. He had escaped from the Blizyn camp and became involved in underground war activities. His first wife and his son perished in Treblinka. He told Regina that two of her other brothers-in-law also survived. Initially, Noah took my mother and grandmother back to Tomaszów, but they knew they had to get out of Poland.

Noah was a mechanic and got his hands on a green convertible that he repaired. My mother dubbed it "the frog." Noah, his new wife Hania, Regina, and Rutka piled into the car and drove three hundred miles to a German border, where Noah bribed a guard at the waterway between Poland and Germany to get them crossed over in a rubber raft. They camped in the woods on that first night. In the darkness, Regina stumbled and broke her arm. It couldn't be set until they reached Berlin a few days later.

They eventually ended up in a displaced persons camp in Feldafing, Germany. Feldafing had been a resort area where wealthy people from Munich had country homes, most of which were destroyed during the war. They would spend three years there.

In Feldafing, there was both an overt grapevine and an underground grapevine. The underground grapevine comprised of survivors desperately trying to find out if their family members survived. The overt grapevine was essentially a match-making service. The complicated process of rebuilding fractured lives had begun. Couples were formed and began to get married. In Feldafing, most of these unions were not first marriages. Then, the babies started being born.

In 1946, my grandmother married Jack Cymberg in Feldafing. I believe Jack was also from Tomaszów, but they hadn't known each other there. My ten-year-old mother was not at the ceremony. In fact, she wasn't even told about it until after they were married. It was a huge adjustment to have this new man in her life, and my mother used to tell me that she was very angry about it at the time. My mother had been the sole focus of Regina's attention, and she was not interested in vacating that position.

Jack's life had also been decimated by the war. He survived Dachau and Bergen-Belson, but lost his wife and two children.

He was a talented tailor by profession and always dressed immaculately. He took enormous pride in his appearance. For a long time, my mother only called him "Mr. Cymberg." Eventually, my mother and Jack became close. He was very good to both my mother and my grandmother. They were truly a family.

My grandmother became pregnant in Feldafing but miscarried. My mother once told me that she had been relieved that there wasn't going to be a baby. She never elaborated on why, but I assume she was worried that she would be replaced.

Now they needed to figure out where to go. My mother wanted to go to Palestine, but the British had been turning back ships. Montreal wanted tailors as the needle trade was very big there, and so, they applied. They made frequent trips to Munich to get the required documentation, but they kept getting their Canadian Visa applications turned down. There was great fear they wouldn't get in.

They finally made it to the next stage and were given physicals. One step closer. My mother's X-rays showed lung lesions. Tuberculosis. They all assumed that this would stop the process but, for some reason, somebody chose to overlook it, and they were granted Visas to Canada.

They boarded a ship in Hamburg, leaving shattered lives behind to face a new and uncertain future. It was a long and difficult transatlantic journey, and they were seasick for much of it. They arrived in Halifax, Canada in January of 1948, and then taken by train to Quebec. The first stop was some sort of holding facility just outside of Montreal. My mother noted that the community was exceptionally well-organized and welcoming.

She was now eleven years old and went by the name Rachel Cymberg. Once processed, the survivors were put on a bus bound for the city. She remembered driving by St. Lawrence Street for the first time. Her eyes lit up as she passed the shops and restaurants. She had never seen anything like it. She said it felt like being liberated again. As an adult, my mother loved going back down to St. Lawrence Street in January, even if it was bitterly cold. It made her happy.

My mother's family initially lived in the spare room of a Canadian family's apartment. There were a lot of survivors clustered in the area, including people from Tomaszów. They would get together to play cards on Saturday night. It was the only time they talked about their wartime experiences. They felt that no one who was not there could possibly understand. In that community, my mother was the only child.

My grandmother asked the Jewish Immigrant Aid Society about a Hebrew day school for my mother, and they found her a spot. It was a private school, but admission was waived for Holocaust survivors.

My mother was still eleven years old when she started grade one. They had to bring in a bigger desk for her as she didn't fit in the pint-sized desks made for six-year-olds. The school also provided her with private lessons.

My mother was keenly aware that she was not like the other Canadian children. She wore her hair in two long braids, couldn't speak English, and dressed differently. Jack made her clothes, which included a pair of leggings sewn from a navy-blue blanket to keep her warm in the frigid Montreal winter. At some point, my grandmother cut off my mother's braids, but she kept them in a drawer. I was fascinated by those braids when I was a child and always asked to see them whenever I visited my grandmother's apartment. They were still intact, chopped off at the top with the ribbons still tied at the bottom.

My mother was a quick learner and went through six grades in three years. By the time she graduated with her cohort in grade six, she spoke English, French, Hebrew, and Yiddish. Those first years in Canada are probably when my mother figured out that looking like everyone else was the perfect camouflage for hiding her past. Dressing well and fitting in became very important to her. Later, after she had me, I was mandated to continue that tradition. How I presented to the world was a reflection on my mother and her ability to assimilate.

She was social, outgoing, good at sports, and made friends easily. All her friends were Canadian-born. She was tall for her age and joined the basketball team, which also helped her integrate. She once broke her nose when she was hit in the face by a basketball. It was never fixed properly, so she developed a bump on her nose that never went away. But she was still beautiful.

Jack and Regina spoke in heavily accented English. My mother had no accent. As far as I know, they were happy. They were hard workers, and were eventually able to afford their own apartment.

After high school, my mother studied to become a nurse. Another step in her journey to becoming fully integrated into Canadian society.

My mother and I didn't discuss her wartime experiences very much, but she did tell me repeatedly that she disliked the word "survivor." It was not how she wanted to be defined. She felt that she was simply born at the wrong time and place. Surviving was an accident, not a virtue. She clung to the notion that her childhood wasn't that bad. She had felt loved and protected. She claimed that lots of people had tougher childhoods than her.

Yet, she also acknowledged that she was scarred by her experiences. That sometimes she could deal with her traumatic past, while other times, anxiety and fear would overwhelm her. She'd tell me that she did not want to "drag her past around like a sack of potatoes." She didn't hide her tattoo, but it made her very uncomfortable when people asked about it. She wanted to be undetectably Canadian and fit into the fabric of society.

To me, "survivor" is a misnomer. We speak of surviving as if it were the ultimate victory, when it is, in fact, just the beginning of a lifelong battle. As an adolescent, when I peeked into my mother's bedroom during those long daytime naps, I saw that she slept with her arm over her eyes, as if she was still blocking out some slideshow of horror. It was an extremely disturbing image.

If you are born into a family that isn't fatalistic, then you might actually believe that once the worst has happened, it is over. You are safe. But my mother knew differently. She had seen for herself that something worse than the worst was possible. Black clouds are always speeding across the horizon. Safety is just an illusion.

Her omnipresent fear had a profound impact on those closest to her. Her past was a dominating force in our present.

Rachel and Brahm

MY MOTHER TRANSFORMED HERSELF INTO A typical Canadian teenager. She had friends, she went out, she had boyfriends. Nothing could outwardly betray her past except for the number on her left arm.

She was accepted into the Jewish General Hospital's School of Nursing, starting in the fall of 1955, but found herself at loose ends the summer after she graduated high school. Her stepfather, Jack, was working as a tailor for the English & Scotch Woolen Company. The owner of the shop had recently remarried, and his wife owned a summer camp. My mother got a job there as a camp counsellor. She loved it.

That summer laid the groundwork for her future in the form of Max Palayew. He was a counsellor at the camp, and a few years older than her. Max and my mother didn't interact that summer, but they knew of each other. He was a medical student who later came to play a pivotal role in the lives of my family.

They crossed paths again that September when she began her nursing training. Max was doing his residency in radiology at the same hospital. He was close friends with Brahm Hyams, a surgical resident. Max told Brahm that he should keep an eye out for Rachel Cymberg, a cute, spunky nurse who was a good athlete and whom Max thought would be a good match for him. So Brahm watched her from afar . . . for more than two years.

One night, during her third and final year of nursing training, my mother was doing an 11 p.m. to 7 a.m. shift at the hospital. She was the in-charge nurse for the surgical ward that evening. She had a patient with a perforated gallbladder who had to be prepped for surgery, but she wasn't feeling well. Earlier that day, she'd gone on a date where they spent time out on a boat enjoying the beautiful summer weather, but without a hat, she ended up with sunstroke.

She had a horrible headache, which was affecting her ability to concentrate. She was allergic to aspirin, so she went down to the Emergency Department and asked if it would be possible to get some codeine. Because it was a narcotic, which had to be prescribed and logged, she had to wait for the surgical resident to arrive. Ta da! In walks Brahm Hyams. They chatted briefly, he wrote her the prescription, and she went back to the surgical ward to finish her shift. My father later admitted to her that he was very impressed by her work ethic.

My mother and father continued to bump into each other at the hospital, and she began to suspect that he was interested in her. She wasn't ready for any type of serious involvement. He was six years older than her, and she wasn't that keen on dating a doctor. The graduating nurses felt superior to the interns and residents because they felt that they knew more about patient care than these newly minted doctors. In those days, there was a structured hierarchy in the hospital system. If a doctor came into the nursing station, the nurse had to give up their seat. My mother thought that was ridiculous.

One day at the hospital, as she was getting on an elevator, she spied Brahm in the distance. He jumped in just as the doors closed. On that brief elevator ride, my father asked my mother to accompany him to the upcoming hospital ball. He explained that he was on call that night but that it shouldn't be an issue since the ball was taking place in the hospital. She agreed to go with him.

On the night of the ball, he called her to say that he couldn't pick her up because the Surgeon-in-Chief, Harry Ballon (who was also my father's uncle), brought in an emergency case and he had to be in the operating room to assist. Not wanting to inconvenience my mother, he arranged for a friend and his wife to pick her up.

The evening started with a cocktail party. My mother and the married couple were having a wonderful time, but my father was still in the operating room. He eventually appeared. He had only ever seen my mother in her nurse's uniform, and while he felt she did look cute in it, with its little matching cap, he was not prepared for this vision in a pale blue and lilac print cocktail dress with a crinoline and shoes dyed to match. Dyed to match! He later said he fell hook, line, and sinker right then and there.

By now, my mother was also beginning to be a bit more intrigued by (and attracted to) him as well. My father was not traditionally handsome, but he had sparkling grey eyes and a great sense of humour. He was steadfast, accomplished, and kind. He also came from a "good family." His father was the first Jewish orthodontist in Montreal. I think my mother started realizing that this doctor, every Jewish mother's dream, was a catch.

My mother didn't keep very many of her old clothes, but I remember seeing that cocktail dress many times when I still lived at home. It hung in what we called the "second closet" in the basement (the first closet was filled with toys and stuffed animals from my childhood, but the second seemed to be just a hodgepodge of random things). I always wondered why she kept that dress but never thought to ask her. It wasn't until the dress was long gone, discarded in the household purge after her death, that I learned the significance of that blue and lilac dress. I long to have that dress back. To have a memento of my parent's first date.

Their relationship progressed very quickly, but my father was conflicted. He would soon be moving to Des Moines, Iowa, to finish his surgical training and he didn't see the point of continuing to date seriously. But, he had already fallen for her.

One day after work, six weeks after the hospital ball, my father drove my mother home to the apartment she shared with her parents. He didn't come in because he was expected at his own parents' house for dinner. Soon after he dropped her off and continued on his way, the little car he'd purchased from his sister for $100 got stuck in a snowbank and wouldn't budge. Since he was only a few blocks away, he trudged back through the snow to my mother's apartment.

My mother was exhausted after a long shift, already in bed in her flannel nightgown when he returned. After calling his parents to tell them he couldn't make it for dinner, my father went into her bedroom, sat on the edge of the bed, and asked her a question: "Would you come to Iowa with me?"

She responded, "Well, would you marry me?"

My father was both amused and taken aback. "You're not supposed to ask me. I'm supposed to ask you." So, he did. And she accepted. That was on the thirteenth of February. They were married on June 10, 1959, less than six months after their first date. And off they went to Des Moines, Iowa.

They were a typical young married couple. My father was working long hours at the hospital where my mother also worked as a nurse. In black-and-white photographs from those years, they seem very happy. Smiling and laughing, digging their car out of the Midwest snow, vacationing with my grandmother Regina and her husband Jack at a beach.

Three years after my parents moved to Des Moines, Jack died of a massive coronary at age fifty-seven. At only forty-seven, my grandmother was now twice widowed. Her parents, first husband, and siblings had all died in the Holocaust. What I have since come to understand is that there are some extraordinary people in this world who can somehow make it through that much trauma without being destroyed by it. My grandmother was one of those people.

My paternal grandfather, Ben Hyams, also died of a heart attack later that year at the age of sixty-three.

In 1962, after four years in Des Moines, my father completed his training and they moved back to Montreal. He opened a surgical practice, and my mother stopped working to prepare for the next phase of their lives.

Later that year, my mother became pregnant with me. Doctors discovered a mass in her abdomen and couldn't determine if it was malignant or benign. My parents were given a choice: surgery now and lose the baby, or wait until the baby was born to have the surgery. They decided to wait. How terrifying it must have been for them to be experiencing the joy of a first baby and a potentially life-threatening issue for my mother at the same time.

She had the surgery a few days after I was born. To remove the mass, the surgeon had to cut into her stomach muscles, so she always had a scar, and a small pot belly. The mass was benign.

I was born on May 8, 1963, on the eighteenth anniversary of Victory in Europe Day (V-E Day). In Jewish tradition, the number eighteen is significant because it represents the Hebrew word "chai," meaning life, and symbolizes good fortune. My father's last name, Hyams, is also derived from the word chai. When my father's ancestors arrived from Europe, their last name was Brejesky. As was typical in those days, the Canadian authorities suggested they adopt a more "Canadian-sounding" name. They settled on Hyams. While it is a lovely connection, let me tell you, no one can pronounce it or spell it properly. Also, they clearly never considered that it was a little too close to "hymen," which often sent my high school classmates into paroxysms of laughter.

If you believe in signs from the universe, which I do, it's hard to summarily dismiss the significance of a baby being born from the ashes of Auschwitz on that date.

There was a study done on Holocaust survivors suggesting that the trauma they suffered can actually alter their DNA. Transgenerational epigenetic inheritance theorizes that external influences, like extreme stress, can affect the genes of your children and even grandchildren. I became my parents' first child, my grandmother's first grandchild, and possibly the proud new owner of trauma-altered genes.

I understand how my father fell in love with my mother. She was bright, vivacious, fun. I truly believe that the first four years of their marriage were happy and uneventful. Everything changed after I was born.

Welcome to Anxiety 101

THE PROBLEM WITH COMING FROM A FUCKED-UP FAMILY is that by the time you recognize the reality of your situation, it's too late . . . you are already fucked up. When I was young, I thought our family life was normal. Because I had never known anything else.

My mother was living a life that was light-years away from the Holocaust. She was qualified as a nurse, married to a doctor, had two kids, and lived in a nice house in an upscale neighbourhood. She put up a very normal front, but she lacked the emotional and physical stamina to manage this life. Her past trauma was harder to bury under the pressure of parenting and trying to navigate our family through the type of life she had never had.

As a mother, I know that having a child changes your mindset forever. What if I somehow fail to keep this child safe? What if they get seriously ill? These very normal parental feelings were magnified for my mother. My grandmother Regina, now dubbed "Bubby," played a huge role in my upbringing. It was all hands on deck. Protecting me was a matter of life and death for both of them. There was a lot riding on my survival. As they knew, safety was not guaranteed. Bad things can happen anywhere, even when there is no war going on.

My mother's childhood meant she had no exposure to what a traditional childhood looked like. She had to learn about "normal" families in a vacuum. She had nobody to look to for examples of typical parent-and-child dynamics. Other than my grandmother, she had no blood relatives on that side of the family, and the few remaining members of her father's family were not in Canada.

So, she bought child-rearing books. Lots of them. This was always her default. When she felt she didn't have the tools to deal with a situation, she read. She also carefully observed her friends who were already mothers and bombarded them with questions.

She worried that her past would impact on her ability to be a good wife and mother. Since she'd arrived in Canada, her primary objective had been to look and act like everybody else. But when she had me, she realized that she was, indeed, different. Her carefully constructed façade of "being just like everybody else" was in danger of crumbling.

I noticed the cracks starting to show when I was around four years old. My mother had enrolled me in a plethora of activities following the lead of her friends with young children. She was perpetually running late, which made her anxious and, in turn, angry at me. There was often screaming (her) and tears (me). By the time we arrived at Gabor Bartha's music class, the MUST-attend toddler music program, I was usually a pint-sized nervous wreck.

Of course, I ended up in dance ("perfect daughters dance"). I loved the pink cupcake-ness of ballet. I was good, a quick learner pushed by a streak of get-out-of-my-way competitiveness. But my hair was a huge issue for my mother. I had long, stringy, oily hair that tangled easily. It refused to be corralled into a beautiful bun. This would throw my mother into a rage. If only she had known about conditioner, I would have had a much happier childhood.

I had my first ballet recital when I was five. My mother and the bun were engaged in a fierce battle, so when we finally made it to the recital, we were late. My mother saw that a group of children were already performing so she literally pushed me into the middle of the performance. I just stood there. Mortified. This wasn't my group. The ballet teacher eventually took me by the hand and brought me back to my mother, explaining that my group was the next to perform. I was furious at my mother and burning with humiliation, but my love of ballet persevered. I borrowed every book about ballet from the school library, marvelling at the elegance of the world's best ballerinas and absorbing the message: to be beautiful, you must be thin.

My mother started taking me to see ballet productions. Sometimes she brought my grandmother as well. It was on one of these occasions that my mother had an epiphany while we were descending the escalator after a performance at Place des Arts (Montreal's version of Lincoln Center). There is a very strong resemblance between the three of us, and we looked like three beautifully dressed Matryoshka nestling dolls, one smaller than the other. It suddenly struck her that this moment was a triumph. We looked like everybody else in this well-heeled crowd. A young child, her mother, and her grandmother, who all blended in seamlessly. We were indelible proof that Hitler failed. That evil does not always triumph. But evil does have a long reach.

There was a litany of things that drew my mother's laser-like focus on me. She hated being cold, but it was more than that. It was almost as if she had a pathological fear of the cold. Maybe it reminded her of that freezing winter in Auschwitz. She became the defender of my warmth.

Halloween in Montreal was always frigid, and my mother insisted that I wear a snowsuit underneath my costume. At age six, I was very excited about dressing up as Raggedy Anne, but once my adorable costume had been stretched over my snowsuit, I looked like a small, bizarrely bloated creature that escaped from a horror movie set. I was miserable. My mother had a knack for turning simple childhood activities into outlets for her anxiety.

We weren't allowed to trick-or-treat at houses where she didn't know the people. After visiting a few neighbours, we would drive to my father's sister's house. Aunt Ruthie's daughters, Charlotte and Sandi, were a few years older than me, and I idolized them. We sat in their warm living room eating the candy meant for trick or treaters. A few years later, I finally convinced my mother to allow me to go trick-or-treating with my friends. She assumed their parents accompanied them. Of course, my friends weren't supervised by their parents. They were allowed to go out on their own, to ANY house they wanted. And they didn't have to wear snowsuits under their costumes!

The battle around what I wanted to wear was not limited to Halloween costumes. In those days, party dresses were worn with white frilly ankle socks and patent leather Mary Jane shoes, but when I looked in the mirror, I thought my legs looked plump and out of proportion. I was pocket-sized, and my legs were twigs, but I insisted on wearing black tights instead. Those ankle socks were the enemy. My mother, understandably, could not comprehend my aversion. Plus, it ruined what she considered the appropriate attire for a six-year-old. I won the battle about fifty percent of the time.

The summer after I turned seven, my parents rented a country house in Trout Lake, an hour outside of Montreal. Bubby stayed with us as well. It was a magical place. We swam in the cold lake and would walk to Belisle's, the corner store, every night to get ice cream cones.

My father would commute from the city, staying overnight on Wednesdays and on weekends. He taught me how to ride a bike there. I remember the exact moment I mastered it, with my father directing me to "KEEP PEDALLING" as I manoeuvred the lawn. Euphoria!

But bikes in the city were deemed too dangerous by my mother. I wasn't allowed to ride mine once we returned home. When I outgrew my childhood bicycle, I was never allowed to get another one.

The owners of the house we rented in Trout Lake lived next door. They had four daughters who were close to me in age. The owner's eldest daughter and I were allowed a certain measure of freedom, roaming the forested grounds on the property looking for toads.

At eight, I begged my mother to be allowed to go to the day camp that was just down the road. She was not keen on it but eventually relented. That first summer, she walked me to camp every morning and picked me up in the afternoon.

The next summer, I wanted to walk the short distance to camp on my own but my mother had tremendous anxiety about my physical safety. My grandmother had saved her daughter's life when they were in imminent danger. This was what my mother witnessed, and that is what she emulated. But we weren't in Auschwitz; we were in a bucolic, safe place. I had no perspective on why she was trying to control every aspect of my existence. I only knew that I was starting to chafe at what I perceived to be her amplified parental control. In this case, I won the battle. Joy! My tiny feet kicking up dust as I traversed the seven-minute walk on my own. I felt freedom in every step.

As it turned out, it was not physical safety that was my biggest problem that summer. While my thin frame and elongated neck may have been a ballet ideal, it earned me the nickname "ostrich" from a vicious little girl in my bunk. This was my first brush with being bullied. It was far from the last.

In the heat of the summer, my mother and grandmother often wore sleeveless tops. I noticed their number tattoos and asked my mother about them. I was given the age-appropriate explanation that they had been in the Second World War. I was eight, the same age as my mother when she received the tattoo.

The Holocaust was confusing to me. It was something both known and unknown in our lives. My mother rarely talked about what she'd been through, and she would tell anyone who would listen that her childhood was no worse than anyone else's. This was the "Big Lie." And we all had to play along and pretend that her history had no impact on her, even though we lived with the fallout day after day.

Throughout my childhood, my mother's anxiety continued to seep into my life, in both big and little ways. It was the omnipresent soundtrack playing in the background.

We were at cross purposes. She was trying to keep me safe. I was trying to grow up. Then I learned what she was so scared of. One day, I overheard my parents discussing in hushed tones an accident that happened to the child of someone they knew. Nine-year-old Laurie Slapcoff was walking on the sidewalk with a friend, when a student driver jumped the curb and hit her. I kept asking my dad if she was okay. A few days after the accident, she passed away. That was the day I learned what my mother already "knew."

That death may be peeking around every corner waiting to claim us. That the natural order of the universe could be upended, and children could die before their parents. That my mother would never survive the loss of a child. And thus, the seeds of anxiety were sown. One day, I would have children. If I wasn't already carrying a genetic predisposition for anxiety, the environmental factor was unavoidable.

My mother was likely unaware of how her past was informing my present. In retrospect, I realize that I, too, was manifesting behaviours rooted in fear.

From the time I was a little girl, I was obsessed with stuffed animals. There were a dozen or so that I slept with every night. They had to be lined up in a specific order before I got into bed. I thought if they weren't in the proper position, something bad would happen. Happen to who? To me? To my family? I wasn't sure, but I knew that I couldn't risk it.

I was also always careful to not let my arms or legs hang over the edge of the bed. This would prevent the evil forces lurking under it from grabbing me and carrying me off into the darkness. I still sleep that way.

My mother's fears continued to reveal themselves as if they were locked in a steamer trunk until she was ready to take them out. Like Pandora, once freed, they could never be contained again. Her anxiety clung to me from birth, although I was not aware of it until much later.

My mother devised clever ways to insert herself into my life. When I was in elementary school, she came up with the perfect cover to keep me under her watchful gaze. She began volunteering as the nurse at my school. She eventually became "head nurse" of the program. If I was being generous of spirit, which I sometimes had difficulty being around my mother, I could have interpreted this as a way that a bored housewife with time on her hands was able to make a valuable contribution to society.

She had a variety of duties. At Field Day for grades four to six, there was my mom, taking care of skinned knees. Everyone loved her . . . the students, the teachers, and the principal. I was so proud to be her daughter. I felt like a mini celebrity. But in addition to handing out band-aids and taking temperatures, my mother was also responsible for sex education, which began in grade four.

WHAT THE FUCK!

I did not want to sit through a class where my mother described how babies were made, even if it was very abstract in those early grades and mostly involved chickens' reproductive systems. Still, I dreaded the days she came to my class. It actually wasn't too horrific in grades four and five, but the worst was yet to come.

My mother thought it would be a great idea to have my father, the doctor, come in for the grade six session and provide the definitive guide to human procreation. There were one hundred students in my grade. We all filed into the library and sat on the itchy carpet. My mother spoke first and introduced my father. He smiled and waved at me. Here we go. My father uttered the words penis and vagina. Ninety-nine heads swivelling in unison to look at me. I don't think either of my parents appreciated how humiliating this was for me. And it wasn't a one-off. My parents tag-teamed these presentations for years, so literally thousands of students at my elementary school were privy to them. It still comes up in conversation with people who were students at that time. Yes, I'm still embarrassed all these decades later.

I was starting to suspect that my friends' mothers were not as overbearing in their lives as my mother was in mine. They didn't seem to be embroiled in the daily battles that I was.

By fifth grade, my friends were allowed to take the city bus to school. I still rode the school bus. Heading into grade six, I decided there was no fucking way I was riding the school bus anymore. I was the oldest kid on the bus. The school bus and the city bus dropped off their passengers in the same place, so everybody could see I was taking the school bus. I told my mother I absolutely refused to ever get on the school bus again. My father intervened and insisted I was old enough to take the city bus on my own.

While I won that battle in a direct confrontation, there were others that I lost, forcing me to take matters into my own hands. My mother was still insisting I wear snowsuits. My friends had long since ditched theirs, replacing them with trendy bomber jackets. She would not even entertain it. A jacket that only went to my waist was a guaranteed recipe for pneumonia. Since she was in charge of making those purchases, we seemed to be at a standoff.

One year, she bought me a particularly hideous two-piece snowsuit, bright yellow with bright blue piping. When I arrived at school, my friends made fun of me. From that day forward, as soon as I was out of her line of sight and before I got on the city bus, I took off the snow pants and stuffed them into my knapsack. Same with the taupe knit hat that had a scarf attached to it that my friends laughed at. Crisis averted. Sort of. I was in fact freezing and did get sick a lot. She just never knew why.

Conflicts with my mother weren't the only source of unrest in my house at that time. Despite the fact that my father was a successful surgeon with a thriving practice, he was very unhappy in his career. He had fought so hard to become a doctor in a time when there were quotas limiting the number of Jewish medical students, but he was too compassionate and psychologically unable to create the professional distance that surgeons need to have with their patients.

While conducting research for the book, Eunice Palayew, Max's wife and a close friend of both my parents, told me that my father became very depressed and considered giving up medicine. He did not like to disappoint people, and his decision was further complicated by the fact that he was a member of The Ballon and Goldbloom families, who were high profile in Montreal's small Jewish community. Eunice felt that my father would have had a very hard time telling his uncle Harry, still the Jewish General's Surgeon-in-Chief, that he no longer wanted to be a surgeon and that he was considering leaving medicine.

Once again, it was Max who swooped in to play a pivotal role in my parents' life. Max was a radiologist and convinced my father to switch to this specialty. This required him to do a second residency at nearly forty years of age. When he began this residency, I was around eight. Eunice says that her perception of my mother at that time was that she was incredibly supportive of my father as he made that career transition and that she was the one holding the family together. I remember it differently.

My father was on call a lot. This meant my mother was shouldering the lion's share of childcare duties, which now included my six-year-old brother.

When my father was home, which wasn't often, my mother was usually yelling at him. She couldn't handle the pressure of parenting on her own, and getting angry at my father was the release valve. While I didn't see her as terribly supportive of him, any support he did receive during this difficult period may partially explain his loyalty to her. Other than the yelling, life was okay. We would visit my dad at the hospital and stop into the tiny room where he slept when he was on call. There was a human skeleton in the closet which I remember thinking was hilarious. I didn't realize at the time that there were also skeletons in the closets at home, too.

Because of my father's second residency, we couldn't afford to take family vacations, but my mother had relatives on her father's side in New York who we would occasionally visit. One year, my father thought it would be great fun to take an overnight train. A train? Really, dad? Needless to say, my mother was not enthusiastic about the idea of being on a train again. My father booked a sleeper car with bunk beds. My mother and I slept together on the extremely narrow top one, my father and brother on the equally narrow bottom one.

Turns out that it is exceedingly difficult to get a good night's sleep on a train. There is a lot of jostling, and when you pass another train, its lights illuminate the cabin and the wheels make a high-pitched squeal. We were basically up all night, with my mother yelling at my father about what a stupid idea it was.

She said it was the tracks rather than the train cars that she found so upsetting. They seemed to go on into infinity. She always experienced a moment of shock when she first saw the tracks, transporting her immediately back to Auschwitz. It took tremendous effort on her part to bring herself back to the present. She had that visceral reaction every time she got on a train.

By the time I turned ten, my father was on sound financial footing and we started taking proper family vacations. It quickly became clear that travel in general was a huge problem for my mother. My grandmother also played a role in that. She gave my mother shit about how much money she was spending on something frivolous and how irresponsible it was for all of us to risk our lives by flying. My mother could not handle being criticized by her mother. She was wedged between her mother's anxiety and her husband and children's excitement about taking a trip. There was always a battle royale the night before we left, with my mother insisting that we weren't going, while I cowered in my bedroom.

Things usually did not improve once we made it to our chosen destination. I loved staying in hotels—staying up late with my parents watching TV, the endless breakfast buffet—but inevitably, my mother would find problems. As soon as the elevator door to our floor would open and we would trudge down the hall to our room, the complaints began: "Our room is too close to the noisy elevators." "The ice machine is right next door." Back down to the lobby we would go to request a room change.

Once we had been reallocated to a new room, my father was always keen to start exploring our new destination. My mother did not move at the same pace. "Brahm, you are trying to jam too many activities in."

My parents fought nearly every night on vacation, to the point where other guests would call security because of the screaming. Hotel security knocking at the door telling my parents to keep it down was commonplace. We always stayed in a single room, so I was trapped. I have battled insomnia since I was a child, and in these cramped quarters, I had nowhere to go when I couldn't sleep. My mother instructed me to go read in the unfilled bathtub, so I didn't disturb anyone. Family trips were joyless.

Like many Montrealer's, Florida was our destination of choice for winter vacations. On one of our trips to Florida, my mere existence seemed to be a constant source of irritation to my mother. I was trying to interact with her as little as possible so I asked if I could buy a book at the airport to read on the plane. She looked at the assortment in the bookstore and pulled out *The Bad Seed* by William March, about an eight-year-old sociopath who inherits a murderous gene from her grandmother. I was ten years old. But she was right, I loved the book.

One year, there was a massive snowstorm predicted on the day we were supposed to fly to Miami. Montreal snowstorms are not to be trifled with. My father decided we would have a better chance of making our morning flight if we stayed at an airport hotel the night before. My mother was not in agreement. If the weather was bad, she did not want to risk flying. The fighting started before we left for the hotel and continued all night. Between their screaming and the noise of the snowploughs, no one got any sleep. We did, however, manage to get on our flight.

The worst family trip was Disney World. My mother didn't want to go, but my father and I were so excited that she eventually relented. When we got to the park, my mother instantly became agitated. She later said she didn't know why she had that reaction, but she hated every minute of it. On top of that, we were not a daredevil-ride-loving family. In fact, we were probably the most ride averse people in the park. *It's a Small World* was our favourite. My father, trying to mitigate what was quickly becoming another unpleasant family vacation, agreed to ride the Alice in Wonderland whirling teacups with me. He was nauseous for the rest of the day. We were one and done at Disney.

Years later, my mother read *The Book of Daniel* by E.L. Doctorow. In it, he describes the crowd control at Disney World and the parallel between how Disney managed this and how the Nazis processed people in the camps.

As an adult, that all makes sense to me. How could she *not* feel that way after everything she had been through? But as a child, just trying to enjoy the Magic Kingdom, her panic and out-of-control behaviour ruined the trip for all of us. She did a terrible job of hiding her misery, so that really added to the fun of "the happiest place on earth."

Her fear of crowds, lining up, and parades became a recurrent theme. My private Jewish elementary school often participated in marches to support various Jewish causes. She never wanted me to go but I insisted. Like my mother, I, too, wanted to blend in.

Life with my mother was like having a chronically sick child in the family. We were always off balance; our energy tilted toward her. All the attention sucked into her vortex. Screaming. Door slamming. Weeping. Piling on the guilt. Even when she withdrew, shutting her bedroom door and closing out the daylight for hours, she held us hostage with her absence. We tiptoed around like eggshell people, waiting for her to re-emerge, dreading the inevitable tirade. Our breaths held, waiting for the other fashionable shoe to drop.

My father was the polar opposite of my mother. While she was standing up in the lifeboat waving her arms wildly and making us feel like she was going to capsize us, he was always trying to calmly navigate. She rocked; he steadied. All my life, he had let me know the world wasn't always terrifying. And he made me feel that I deserved a place in it. He was my shelter from the storm.

We were still living in an upper duplex while all my mother's friends had bought houses. A lot of things did not feel to my mother like they were going according to plan. I was ten when we moved into the red brick house on a corner lot in Westmount. My father grew up in that neighbourhood and he was very proud that he'd become successful enough to buy a house there.

The second residency may have delayed my parents' plans to buy a house, but once they did, it quickly became my mother's showpiece. She worked with a designer to transform the dated décor into a beautiful home. My mother had great taste and was bold in her choices.

She took down a wall in the kitchen to create the huge bright orange, navy, and white masterpiece kitchen. The living room walls were painted a deep matte burgundy and accessorized with bold floral print sofas. The navy dining room wallpaper worked beautifully with the high polish mahogany table for twelve where she entertained. But my favourite was the main floor powder room. Opening its sliding doors revealed art deco wallpaper and an Aubrey Beardsley print. My mother loved art deco (as do I). We should have been a happy family in this beautiful house. And to the outside world, we appeared to be.

Never Pretty Enough

MY MOTHER LOVED VOGUE MAGAZINE. She was a loyal subscriber. At her behest, I started reading it with her when I was nine years old. We would sit together at the kitchen table, and she would tell me about the designers featured on the glossy pages. She knew all the names of the models. Her favourite was Karen Graham from the Estée Lauder ads. The fact that the models were all skinny did not escape me.

We tracked the rise of the early supermodels. The *Sports Illustrated* swimsuit issue cover, with Cheryl Tiegs in a mesh bathing suit, set an impossible standard. I prayed for "big boobs," but my body did not comply. My favourite model was Kelly Emberg, maybe because she was a bit unusual-looking and had buck teeth like me. My mother affectionately called me her "buck-toothed wonder." This only added to my insecurity. I still smile with my mouth closed.

One day in the car, buckled into the back seat, I asked my mother, "Am I pretty?" She glanced in the rearview mirror and hesitated. "Well, you're a type." I was ten years old, and it was clear to me that being "a type" was not the same as being pretty. I so wanted to be pretty, but I was just not one of those genetically blessed girls. My teeth were too big for my face. I was flat-chested. My hair was a disaster. I understood that I did not fit into the narrow description of what my mother, and now I, consider pretty.

I know that my mother always wanted me to be more popular and pretty than I was. I felt she somehow held me responsible for my shortcomings in these areas. She constantly found flaws in my physical appearance, making me feel badly about my acne-prone skin. She never came out and said it, but a steady stream of skincare products would magically appear in my bathroom.

I, in turn, became exacting about her physical flaws. All the models had flat stomachs and my mother did not, because of the surgery that she had after I was born. Everything about my mother was petite and contained except for that little pot belly that always bothered me. My mother wore clothes that hugged her slim silhouette and looked great on her, but the bump, that bump, was always there. And to me, it was awful. I frequently told her that she should be doing sit-ups. I know I made her feel badly about it.

I developed my own fixation with having a flat stomach. The more concave, the better. The best was if your hip bones jutted out. The older I get, the harder it is to maintain a flat stomach. It is an ongoing battle. But that doesn't stop me from standing sideways in front of a mirror, hiking up my top, and assessing my stomach. Several times a day.

As an adult, I am frequently asked how I stay so thin. I respond, "I only eat when I'm happy." The reaction is always the same. A nod of agreement . . . followed by the realization of the meaning of what I'd said. That I must not be happy very often.

My mother had very specific views about the social circle she wanted me to fit into, just as she did when she arrived in Canada and burrowed herself into the landscape of Canadian-born kids. She imparted her terror of "not belonging to the right group" to me. I was made very aware that how I presented to the world reflected on her, and it was clear that I was not meeting her expectations. I sorted out early that there was a direct link between being pretty and being popular.

From a young age, I was overly invested in my social life. I saw school as a necessary evil that interrupted my social activities. Huddling with friends in the schoolyard at recess. Chatting at lunch. I was just like a regular kid, with no one telling me what to do or criticizing me.

In grade six, we had assigned homeroom classes, so your friends tended to be the ones in your class. Melanie and Wendy were my best friends in the class. We ranked about mid-tier in terms of popularity.

We did everything together and spent weekends sleeping at each other's houses. Then, they suddenly dropped me. I was ejected from our trio. Permanently. I never found out why, but it was a teachable moment. I would do everything in my power to never let that happen to me again.

Already insecure about fitting in, I was devastated. I felt I had to hide it from my mother. She would want to know what I did to find myself in this predicament. After this, I became friendly with a group of very unpopular girls. Girls I would not normally have given the time of day to before my other friends dropped me. They were lovely girls. One of them had a farmhouse where we went to celebrate her birthday. We spent hours in the barn, jumping off the upper level into a haystack. I was unpopular but happy.

As it turned out, the most popular girls in the grade were also in my homeroom class. I was hyperaware of these "cool girls," and so was my mother, frequently inquiring about them by name. Even though I was not a part of their clique, I was invited to their parties, which was a partial victory. I'm not sure why I was allowed into their rarified world, but those girls were always nice to me. My mother and I would dedicate a significant amount of time to figuring out what I would wear and blow-drying my hair.

Co-ed parties had built-in minefields—slow dances. Would you be asked to dance, or stand in the corner while everyone else swayed to the music? And if you did get asked to dance, how close were you supposed to lean into your partner? I didn't understand for a long time why the boys kept inching their pelvises away from you to avoid boner contact.

The fashion "must-have" at the time were Howick Stars jeans. All the popular girls wore them. They were high-waisted and wide-legged, and you wore them extra-long, so the hems shredded. They were only available in adult sizes and because I was so thin, they were way too big on me. The only way I would be able to wear them was if we bought the smallest adult size and had them altered. My mother refused to do this. Maybe it was the expense, I'm not sure. She desperately needed me to fit in, and wearing what everyone else was wearing was a huge part of that. I clearly absorbed that credo from her.

Then, a children's brand called Playranch came out with their version. Those were the ones I was allowed to get. Does Playranch sound like a brand name that is going to launch you into the stratosphere of tween popularity? I wore them because it was the best option, but I hated them.

At the end-of-schoolyear "popular kids" dance, I did get asked to slow dance. I was relieved. I was not a loser! Then I noticed that the boy who asked me had a giant glob of mustard on his lower lip from the cocktail wiener he'd just consumed. The road to popularity was littered with condiments.

Whichever friend groups I was moving in and out of, Naomi was the constant in my life. We've known each other since birth, as our parents were in the same social circles. When we were little, Naomi was a "tomboy." At my third birthday party, her mother had made her wear a dress. One of my grandmother's friends told her she looked pretty, and Naomi kicked her. She was always feisty.

As adults, Naomi and I looked at our class pictures from elementary school. Those "cool girls" with names like Leslie, Alissa, and Bonnie were gorgeous. Naomi and I looked like gargoyles in comparison.

Howick Star wars aside, my mother loved to take me clothes shopping. We went to fashion shows and scoured the showrooms on Chabanel Street, where Montreal's garment district was situated. Even if my mother was furious at me, which was often and for any number of reasons, nothing interfered with our Saturday morning retail therapy.

I knew on some level that buying me clothes was a substitute for the affection she often couldn't muster. Beautiful clothes to make up for how she treated me. Clothes became our common language, and I became my mother's best fashion accessory.

The High Holidays at our synagogue were an homage to the fall fashion season. No expense was spared to ensure that I made a splash. I was allowed to wear high heels from the time I was twelve. Because I was a dancer, I easily mastered the art of walking in stilettos. The long aisle to our seats was my fashion runway. The need to always look well-dressed comes with a lot of pressure. Like being skinny, it became a part of my persona.

Sitting in the car after one of our shopping excursions, I told my mother that if I ever wore a jean size larger than 26, I was going to go on a diet. She literally flipped out. First, she began threatening to send me to a doctor that treats anorexia. Then she began screaming at me to get out of the car. I thought she was joking but she wouldn't stop yelling, so I got out. She drove off, leaving me in the busy mall parking lot. I was eleven. I watched the car drive away. I was terrified standing there alone, not sure what I should do. She did eventually come back to pick me up. By then I was furious, refusing to speak with her on the way home. I held it together until I reached my bedroom and burst into tears. I never told anyone about that episode.

If you are attractive and well-dressed, you can camouflage the damage underneath. My mother had curated a perfect cover. Tidy exteriors, ragged interiors. That is how we lived.

We were still spending summers at the country house in Trout Lake, but my friends started going to sleep-away camp. Sleep-away camp? This was the perfect escape hatch. After two years of begging, my mother finally allowed me to go when I was eleven. She was miserable in the lead-up to my departure, but I couldn't wait to spend three-and-a-half weeks away from her. The camp was only a ninety-minute bus drive away, but to me, it felt like being on the other side of the world.

I was not homesick for one second. I loved it. The gossiping into the wee hours with my bunkmates, bug-filled overnight camping trips and co-ed activities. Despite the awful food, and the inevitable ear infections I got from swimming in a freezing lake, I revelled in my freedom.

When I came home, I regaled my parents with camp stories. A canoe trip where we almost died navigating the rapids, the time I was the first girl to be asked to dance at the Saturday night social (but I didn't tell them about my first kiss behind a bunk cabin), and that I was the second female lead in the camp production of *Bye Bye Birdie*. Despite the fact that my mother didn't want me to go in the first place, she loved hearing the stories. When I told my parents about swimming across the entire lake, my mother responded with the only joke I ever heard her tell: "At my camp, we didn't have swimming."

Navigating Teenland

FEAR DOMINATED MY MOTHER'S LIFE and, unfortunately for both of us, it did not dominate mine. It would have made my life easier if it did. She was scared of everything outside of the little bubble that she thought she could control. I was desperate to fearlessly experience the world. We were on a collision course.

Life was reasonably okay when I was just a fuzzy little caterpillar, but getting to the other side of the cocoon was hell as I bit my way out so that I could fly away. My adolescence was tumultuous, difficult, monied, and privileged. I was the oldest child and only daughter of a doctor and a nurse. I attended Jewish private school, and my closet overflowed with beautiful clothes. But my mother's trauma was a palpable, ever-present force in my life.

It felt as if my mother was trying to crawl into my skin and live the life she had been denied at my age. At the same time, she was terrified of my emerging independence and sexuality. She rationalized her tirades as the actions of a responsible mother whose duty it was to protect her child. But I knew even then that it was not about protecting me. It was about insulating herself, trying to manage the anxiety that was now linked to me growing up and wanting to put more distance between us. I was in an impossible position, stuck between her needs and navigating the tectonic plate, ground-shifting pressures of high school.

I had not graduated elementary school on the crest of popularity, but in high school, a new social hierarchy emerged. In case you are wondering what happened to that lovely group of girls who saved me from being friendless in the sixth grade, I completely dropped them. Wendy and Melanie were also in the rearview mirror.

I was an opportunist from a young age, always manoeuvring to get closer to what I wanted. The trap comes from believing that there is always more. You can't live in the present because you are constantly looking ahead to the next thing you want. It's a guaranteed recipe for never being comfortable where you are. If I got the carrot that was dangling in front of me, I no longer wanted it. Now I wanted a new carrot. A better carrot. I was in constant competition with myself.

Still smarting from my grade six friend debacle, I threw myself into ensuring that I stayed firmly planted in my new group of girlfriends. That meant doing everything that my friends did. With the exception of Naomi, who was also the daughter of a Holocaust survivor, our friends had very permissive parents. My mother viewed them as irresponsible. This was going to be a problem.

One day when I was around twelve, I was sitting with my mother in our main floor den watching one of Montreal's fierce snowstorms rage through the oversize windows. She shared that this was when she was at her happiest. When her family was forced to hunker down at home. She didn't have to worry about where we were. We were safe. No awareness that maybe her family didn't want to be landlocked. That there were other places that we wanted to be. She was completely sincere about this desire. I found it disturbing. Defying my mother's "idyllic" wish was inevitable. As were the consequences.

Taking the city bus on a Saturday night to Bob's Big Boy, a popular teen hang-out, was definitely not considered safe. So, in place of partaking in those apparently "life-endangering" adventures with my other friends, Naomi and I ate frozen Sara Lee chocolate layer cake and watched TV in my basement (which had spiders that were so big you could actually hear them skittering across the linoleum floor).

It became obvious to us, in our twelve-year-old wisdom, that the only way we could maintain our social status within our group was to lie to our parents. "I'm sleeping at a friend's house" was code for I'm going to a rock concert or decamping to a friend's whose parents were out of town. Both were, of course, strictly forbidden. I never did make it to Bob's Big Boy.

The list of things I hid from my mother continued to grow. If she was going to infiltrate every aspect of what I considered typical childhood activities, then this was my only recourse. If I got caught, so be it. It was worth it.

Another source of freedom was bike riding—only I, of course, did not have a bike. All my friends were whipping around to each other's houses and the corner candy store. Sometimes when I was at a friend's house, if they had a spare bike, I would ride it, but I eventually stopped. I was too scared. They were expert bike riders. I was not, since the last time I owned a bike, I was seven. How would I possibly explain to my mother that I got hurt riding a bike? Or worse, what if I died in a bike accident? My mother would never forgive me. Even when my mother wasn't with me, her fear was a cloud that followed me around like Shleprock on *The Flintstones*.

Grade seven was Bar Mitzvah year, which meant most Saturdays during the school year were dominated by this activity. It was at Michael Fish's Bar Mitzvah that I sampled my first alcoholic beverage. A whiskey sour swiped off the bar. There they were, beautifully lined up; frothy, orange-hued cocktails with a maraschino cherry. I loved everything about them. The taste, how they made me feel, the fact that I was doing something illicit. Eventually, the bartenders at Bar Mitzvahs wised up and the whiskey sours were placed on the back bar out of reach of cocktail-swilling pre-teens.

When my girlfriends started shaving their legs, my mother expressly forbade it. Not to be deterred, I stole a razor from her bathroom. There was no stopping me from having smooth, silky, hair-free legs. I didn't have a lot of body hair to begin with, but the little I did have made me stand out from my girlfriends. Unfortunately, I didn't know you were supposed to use shaving cream or lotion and, with no one to guide me, I just used water. My mother happened to walk into my bathroom, just as I was trying to staunch the bleeding from the cuts all over my legs. She was furious with me, but I had traversed the bridge. There was no going back. She bought me a pack of razors.

This became our dysfunctional pattern. She made me wear snowsuits, so I ditched them and got sick. She wouldn't let me shave my legs, so I cut myself. Realizing that I was going to disobey her, she clamped down harder.

I don't think she realized that she had transmitted to me this overwhelming need to fit in, but that fitting in often ran headlong into her desire to control me. I was doing things that even I thought were unsafe to keep up with my friends. Her overprotectiveness was an invitation to tiptoe further out on a limb.

Unbelievably, at the time, there were no age restrictions on buying cigarettes in Montreal, so of course we tried smoking. Pre-teens cruising the streets of downtown, cigarettes in hand, eliciting horrified stares.

Wisely, when I told her my friends were making fun of my unibrow, she allowed me to get them waxed professionally knowing that my efforts would likely be calamitous.

Then the make-out parties started. I was not invited to the first few and it made me feel very left out. I finally managed to get myself invited to one and proceeded to spend two hours French-kissing with a boy I didn't even like, just so I could join this elite group of spit swappers. When my mother asked about the party, I told her it was fine and avoided mentioning that I spent most of it in a closet.

In the midst of all this teen drama, my parents announced that we were taking a trip to Israel in the spring. It was my grandmother who was the impetus. Noah—my grandmother's brother-in-law who had retrieved my mother and grandmother at Auschwitz—lived in Israel with his family. My grandmother desperately wanted to see them, so we embarked on a two-week "family mission," an organized trip with several other families. The plan was to travel with the group for the first week and then visit Noah and his family for the second.

My mother was on edge the whole time. When the tour bus took us near the border, you could hear gunfire. Sometimes the bus would pick up hitchhiking soldiers in full regalia, including machine guns. I suspect she must have felt that she had deliberately put her entire family in harms way. On some level, I picked up on her anxiety, but I was more interested in hanging out with the other kids my age on the trip.

And then we visited Yad Vashem, the Holocaust Museum in Jerusalem. I had seen these types of horrific Holocaust photos many times before, but it's different when you are confronted with thousands of them all at once. And the objects. Shoes. Glasses. A sweater knit with two sticks from a German soldier's wool socks. I was very worried about my mother and grandmother, monitoring their reactions as they took it all in. It was horrifying enough for people who did not have a direct link to the Holocaust, but for my mother and grandmother, it was devastating. They were ahead of me and exited before I did. It was dark in the museum, and I remember being blinded by the sunlight when I came out. I saw them sitting together on a bench in the stifling heat weeping. It was too much for all of us. I sat on the bench and wept with them.

The second week was completely different. My mother and grandmother were overjoyed to be with Noah and his family as they were to be with us. We stayed in a hotel, but my grandmother stayed with her family. HER FAMILY. These were words that she was very rarely able to invoke. We visited my adult cousins, went to the beach, and, for once, had a perfect family vacation.

I was going back to camp that summer, but I had a decision to make about my ballet training for the upcoming year before I left. I would be required to train four days a week after school. That meant no more hanging out with my friends during the week, and I was too insecure to do that.

If you are going to pursue ballet as a career, there are two paths you can take. Either you have the discipline and passion to get there on your own, or a parent "stage-manages" you. Unfortunately, I lacked the discipline and confidence, and my mother was not a "Dance Mom." She probably figured out pretty quickly that I would likely have to leave home if I was going to study for a professional career. I deeply regret my decision. Would

I have made it? Who knows. At twelve, I took myself out of the running.

I returned to the euphoria of sleep-away camp and had my first summer romance. We were on the same "colour war" team. Colour war was a major multi-day event where campers in the same age group are divided into teams and compete against each other to become the colour war champion. It was intense. You basically spend every waking moment with your team.

On day one of the three-day event, Mr. Summer Camp Romance told me I reminded him of a girl he went to school with. I knew that girl. She was an "A-lister," pretty and popular. I was shocked by the comparison. We began spending time together and soon became a "camp couple." When he went on a canoe trip, he gave me his jean jacket which I slept in. I made him a woodcut of his nickname in arts and crafts. Then he dumped me. He broke my twelve-year-old heart.

When the new school year started, my friends and I were shocked to learn that the entire tier of "A-list" popular kids left to go to public school. A member of the "B-list" group, I suddenly found myself part of the ruling clique. It was a perfect example of being careful what you wish for. Thirteen-year-old girls can be vicious. Our clique was constantly morphing and there was a lot of mean girl behaviour.

I was desperate to be liked by boys. Having a boyfriend gave you social currency. It also was an ego boost, assuming you weren't summarily rejected. Unfortunately, I usually wasn't interested in the boys who liked me. I shot above my "pay grade." Aiming for boys who liked girls who were prettier or more popular. It was a sure-fire recipe for self-esteem disaster. Not only did it lead to a lot of tears, but worse, it made me a target. I was picked on. Maybe those boys sensed my neediness. They made fun of me for being flat-chested. They remarked on my bad skin. One slipped a note into my bra that said "hello" when I fell asleep on a school trip. There was another obvious conclusion that I arrived at as to why these boys didn't like me. I was ugly.

The "beautiful queen bee" (BQB) of my social group had a very cute boyfriend who went to a different school. He came to visit her one day at our school and thought it would be really funny to attach me to her locker by slipping her combination lock through my belt loop. The only way I could free myself was to leverage my weight against the belt loop and rip it. Everyone laughed. I laughed along too, pretending I thought it was hilarious, while I was actually dying inside.

I was often the odd one out, the weak link forcefully pushing my way back in, always searching for a safe space to offset the chaos of my homelife. It didn't matter how mean those boys and girls were to me. At least they noticed me and I was included. Staying in this friend group was worth putting up with it.

As far as my mother knew, everything was hunky dory at school. Only Naomi knew the truth.

The best part about going back to school was shopping for new clothes. My hair, however, continued to be a source of conflict between my mother and me. She hated that I wore it down. She felt it looked unkempt. My mother had beautiful, thick, straight hair that she had blown out every Saturday into a Jackie O bouffant.

I was presented with two options. Cut it short or wear it in a ponytail off my face. I had seen a picture of myself with my hair in a ponytail—hideous. I never told my mother that was why I was refusing to wear one.

And then Dorothy Hamill ruined my life. Hamill, a US skating sensation destined for Olympic gold, became equally famous for her short, layered wedge bob hairstyle that fanned out when she spun through the air. My mother became convinced that this was the ideal hairstyle for me. Off we went to Mitchell's Living Room, a trendy salon in downtown Montreal. An hour later, I was saddled with my own Dorothy Hamill wedge.

I hated it. It was virtually impossible for me to style it into anything that resembled the intended look. I tried Velcro rollers and hot rollers, but nothing worked. And then a glimmer of hope. Farah Fawcett took over the world with her layered flips. I begged my mother to let me cut my hair like Farrah, but she was convinced it would be a disaster. Truthfully, she probably thought it was too sexy. If I didn't fit into the image that she envisioned for me, then she dug in.

So, while all the other girls were constantly "flipping" their layered locks, I was still sporting my Dorothy do. I finally convinced my mother to let me grow my hair out and try a new salon. The BQB had the perfect Farrah flip. She went to Jean-Jacques, the coolest hairstylist in Montreal, so, of course, that's where I wanted to go too. I begged my mother to take me there. She finally gave in.

On appointment day, my mother picked me up from school and drove me to the salon. She was going to run an errand while I was getting my hair cut, but first, she had a serious discussion with Jean-Jacques. NO Farrah flips. The second she left the salon, Jean-Jacques turned to me and said, in his French accent, "It's your hair, do what you want." Farrah Fawcett, here we come. When my mother came to pick me up and saw that Jean-Jacques had willfully disobeyed her, she was furious and yelled at him in front of the whole salon. From then on, until I was twenty, my mother chose my hair salons.

Montreal was a great place to grow up if you were a rebellious adolescent. My friends and I started going to gay discos when we were fifteen. No one asked for ID, even though we must have looked like extras from the movie *Pretty Baby*. My parents thought I was safe and sound at a sleepover. They kept an envelope full of twenty dollar bills hidden in a sweater drawer that I raided whenever I needed funds for my illicit activities.

Innocent-looking private school girl by day, and smoking, drinking, French-kissing wild child by night. If I was not "pretty enough," I was going to hang onto my burgeoning popularity by any means necessary.

While I was busy with my forbidden nocturnal events, my mother was planning my brother's Bar Mitzvah. She was overwhelmed by the planning details, which included a Friday night out-of-towners dinner, the Bar Mitzvah and luncheon, a party for my brother's friends, and a Sunday brunch. Everything had to be perfect.

There was something manic about her behaviour. What she was going to wear for the plethora of activities consumed her. She was still the little girl worried about wearing the wrong clothes. She went downtown, bought a dress, brought it home, and then returned it. After four of these shopping merry-go-rounds, she decided to have something custom-made. A flowy peach linen dress with cream lace details, which tied around her tiny waist. She also had a matching shawl made. On the way home from the dressmaker, my mother somehow lost the shawl. She was inconsolable. *It was just a FUCKING shawl.* And then the universe intervened. Someone found the shawl on our street and miraculously, our address was on it. A good Samaritan saved the day.

I tried to stay out of the house as much as possible. One day, I was invited to go swimming at an indoor pool located in a friend's grandparents' apartment building. Request denied because, and I quote, "If I drowned, it would ruin the Bar Mitzvah."

Because we attended a conservative synagogue, you were not allowed to take pictures on the actual day of the Bar Mitzvah. The work-around was to take family photos in your Bar Mitzvah attire at home, a few days before. On the appointed day, my mother was buzzing around driving me crazy. I hated the outfit she insisted we buy, a white linen skirt suit with a peach floral blouse that colour coordinated with her outfit. And those hideous white wedge-heeled sandals. The photographer kept telling me to smile. I was smiling, just with my mouth closed. I dreaded that those "buck-toothed wonder" pictures of me would hang on the wall of my parent's home for time immemorial. My parents thought I was deliberately trying to sabotage the photo shoot because I jealous of all the attention around my brother. Nope. I was just tired of the endless drama.

For my mother, there was something more to this major family milestone than just ensuring that her Bar Mitzvah was nicer than the ones her friends planned. This was an event underscored by loss. Tangible proof of who was not there to partake in the celebration. Ghosts hovering over her, torturing her with their absence.

If you attend a Jewish high school, you will inevitably run headlong into Holocaust education. Because my mother was one of the youngest children to survive Auschwitz, I had a direct line to the Holocaust that my peers didn't have. Their grandparents may have been there, but not their parents. The Holocaust was taught like it was ancient history. For me, it was my reality.

At the beginning of each class, the teacher pulled down the screen at the front of the classroom and asked a student to turn off the lights. The projector whirred to life, flashing black-and-white images of skeletal concentration camp prisoners in striped shirts, staring at the camera. Bulldozers pushing bodies into graves. A basket with heads in it. I couldn't bear it. What if I recognized someone from my family? I was forced to watch those movies every week. My mother was aware of it. I'm not sure why she didn't intervene.

Finally, I went to the principal, who was a childhood friend of my mother's and knew her history. I asked to be excused from watching those horror films. She said no, it was a part of the curriculum. But I refused to participate in that *Clockwork Orange* scenario, laying my head down on the desk and closing my eyes until the lights were turned back on. You can never unsee those images.

I was also still waging hand-to-hand combat to maintain my social standing. All the girls started getting their periods. But not me. I was very slow to develop. I finally got my period just before my fifteenth birthday. Thankfully, I was not the last girl in the grade to get it. She got a maxi pad stuck to the outside of her locker with a congratulatory note.

I was always keen to sleepover at my friends' houses, welcoming the distance from my mother. One weekend when I was changing clothes, one of the girls noticed that I still did not have pubic hair. I was crowned with the unfortunate nickname "Telly," after Telly Savalas, the bald TV actor who starred in the popular cop show *Kojak*. To my relief, I eventually did get pubic hair. Ironically, I later spent years actively having it removed when, as an adult, Brazilian waxes became a thing.

In an effort to mitigate the pressure cooker of those girlfriends, I became close with another group of girls in my grade. These were no-drama girls. I ping-ponged between the two groups. Since I was staying out late so often, my parents gave me a credit card for emergencies only. They meant life-threatening emergencies. I broadened the definition to include fashion emergencies. Every Saturday, I would head downtown with Lisa, one of the girls from the nice friend group. She and I would spend hours perusing the stores, refuelling on Asian fast food.

One of our missions was searching for sweet sixteen outfits. Sweet sixteen parties were a very big deal in Montreal. When it came to plan my own, my mother wanted to host it in the basement of our house. Granted, it was a decent-sized basement and it could have worked, but I had much grander plans. La Diligence was the go-to restaurant and event space, and that was what I wanted. One of my best friends, Liane, was having hers there. I could not be dissuaded.

My mother was completely frustrated with me and could not contain her anger. She added a new tool to her arsenal. She was so wound up that she couldn't sleep. In the middle of the night, I would hear my parents' bedroom door open, followed by footsteps storming toward my bedroom door which was then violently flung open. She would proceed to tell me that I was a spoiled brat. Why did I think that I was so fancy that the basement wasn't good enough? It was too expensive. No matter how many times my mother came storming into my room at 2 a.m., I never backed down. La Diligence it was.

Though that particular battle was over something frivolous, the midnight tirades endured, materializing whenever conflict arose between us.

Once the party became a reality, my mother was determined to make it a sensation. She hired Phil Bloom, Montreal's top event planner, to convert the space into "Audrey's Disco," complete with a Saturday Night Fever-style light-up dance floor and disco balls suspended from the ceiling.

But what to wear? My mother and I scoured the stores, and then we found it. An electric blue pleated jersey tunic with matching pants. It was fabulous!

You were obligated to have a host for your sweet sixteen. The ideal was to have your boyfriend as host, but I didn't have one. Instead, I asked a good friend, a boy a year older from a different school. Paul was a very attentive host. I loved the party. One hundred of my nearest and dearest hitting the dance floor while the DJ regaled us with everything from "Knock on Wood" to "Heart of Glass."

Sweet Sixteen protocol included having your closest friends coming back to your house after the party to watch you open gifts, followed by a bagel, lox, and cream cheese early morning breakfast. It was in my basement with my friends sitting in a circle that I discovered I had a gift for improv. As I opened the gifts, I started making fun of the bad ones (the people who gave them to me were not there). And my friends laughed. The meaner I was, the more they laughed. Suddenly, I was a great party trick. My friends couldn't wait for me to unleash my vitriol at their sweet sixteens.

Naomi's parents owned a home in Stowe, Vermont that they decamped to every weekend. Because of all the sweet sixteens, she was allowed to stay home. Alone. Of course, Naomi's became the de facto after-party location. Fuck whiskey sours, I graduated to vodka and orange juice, or really bad white wine purchased at the depanneur, Montreal's version of a corner store, that sold alcohol. Montreal was very progressive and indifferent to the age of the consumer.

We would arrive at Naomi's around 1 a.m. and the party usually broke up around four. I lived a half a block away so I would just walk home. Somehow, my mother found out and forbade me to do that walk. Interestingly, she never asked me what the hell we were doing until 4 a.m. I was not going to miss out on the party, so when it was time to go, I would call a taxi, pretend to limp to the car, and apologize for the short ride, blaming it on my fabricated leg injury. If my mother asked, I told her I was coming from a friend's house in a different neighbourhood.

In my last year of high school, the only thing I really cared about was nabbing a boyfriend. Studying for exams would, of course, have been a wiser decision. While I'd dated a few boys in high school, I had never gone beyond the French-kissing stage. My friends were doling out hand-jobs left, right, and centre, and I had never touched a penis.

There was no bigger prize in my teenage eyes than having a boyfriend. You were instantly catapulted into a higher rung of popularity. You were one of "those" girls that boys liked. That made you special.

My mother was conflicted. Having a boyfriend made you more popular, which she wanted for me, but boys also represented a threat. She worried, correctly, that they would have more power over me than she did. And she worried about the spectre of sex. My former sex educator mother went silent on the topic of sex, except to say "don't." She was firmly rooted in the "why buy the cow when you can get the milk for free" camp. My mother's fears went unrealized. The boy I was crushing on was dating one of my best friends.

During this time, I was also harbouring ambitions of going to medical school, but I was doing badly in chemistry and failing physics. I was required to write provincial standardized exams in those courses, so I signed up for a full day crash course tutorial.

I went with a girlfriend who also was considering medical school. When we walked into the classroom, I noticed a boy from another school who'd turned humiliating me into a blood sport over the last few years. He was seated near the front with a group of other boys who I knew. It was not a big room.

I tried to avoid eye contact, but he noticed me come in. In a very loud voice, he yelled out, "Hey slut!" The words bounced off the concrete walls. My friend's head whipped around to look at me. I just shook my head. I sat in that room for six hours feeling too mortified to take in anything that was being taught. FYI, I passed chemistry and failed physics. My friend got a PhD in psychology.

You would think that being on the wrong side of a bully would have made me compassionate, but it didn't. I discovered what the bully already knew. Being mean to other kids gives you some sort of power. I did terrible things.

At sleep-away camp, I dumped powdered detergent onto a bunkmate's sheets and then covered it up with her blanket. I poured shampoo into her running shoes so that when she stepped in the water during a canoe trip, they bubbled up.

I decided it would be hilarious if I pulled down the tube top of a girl in my unit in front of the dining hall where all the campers gathered. Somehow, instead of just pulling it down, I pulled it off completely. There was this poor girl, standing topless in front of hundreds of campers while I was holding her tube top. She covered herself with her hands and ran back to her bunk.

There were other incidents too, just as vicious. I didn't even dislike the girls that I targeted. I was just jockeying for position. I still remember their names. I hope they don't remember mine.

I didn't like the person I was becoming. One day, my friend Lisa pulled me into the stairwell at school and told me that if I was going to keep being such a bitch, I wouldn't have any friends by the end of the day. I was making derogatory comments about my friends' hair and outfits behind their backs, which inevitably got back to them. I was unsympathetic to their teen drama, which seemed trivial to me but not to them. She was right. But she didn't know what was going on at home. No one except Naomi did. My friends only knew that I had an overprotective mother. They didn't know about the late-night tirades. The constant criticism. I felt like there was no safe space. Not at home and not in school, where I was trying to hide my overwhelming insecurities. I clung to the idea that once I was out of high school, I would reinvent myself. Be a better a person. And it was so close to that finish line.

I was a chronic nail biter but that didn't stop me from painting my nails. Unfortunately, I was really bad at doing my nails, which necessitated frequent touch-ups. When my mother would smell the acetone in the nail polish remover wafting from my bathroom, she would stand in the doorway and lecture me about how that chemical had been linked to autoimmune complications. I, of course, ignored her. At twenty-five, I was diagnosed with thyroid disease. Was there a correlation? I don't know, but I now deal with a series of autoimmune complications.

In those last months of high school, we were given an assignment to write a personal essay about ourselves. Mine was titled "The Red Nails." I was wholeheartedly convinced that if I could grow long nails and paint them red, everything in my world would be okay. That this would mean I gained some measure of control over myself. Tangible proof that I was okay. Eventually, I did stop biting my nails and I painted them that perfect red. Nothing changed.

In June, I slipped the bonds of high school. Little did I know at the time that the real world is, in many ways, just a macro version of high school. Or that the issues with my mother would only escalate.

Breaking Free, Sort Of

THE SUMMER AFTER HIGH SCHOOL, I was a junior counsellor (or in camp vernacular, a "JC") at the sleep-away camp I escaped to for years as a camper. Eight weeks away from home. My mother really struggled with that. I was staff there for four summers and it never got easier for her. As a result, it never got easier for me.

Every June, my mother and I would act out the same absurd scene as I prepared for camp. As staff, we were allowed to bring two duffle bags of clothes, but I knew that no one really monitored it. So, I brought seven. In our basement, I would carefully lay out the piles of everything that I felt I would need. For example, green slouch suede boots. And yes, I did wear them.

I would put my large collection of ridiculously skimpy bathing suits in the duffel bag. My mother would take them out. I would pack my cutest outfits, including the most adorable yellow-and-white-striped short-shorts. She would take them out. In went the essential chunky knit sweater for cool evenings. Out it came. We were like Lucy and Ethel on that assembly line with the chocolates. Except she was screaming at me and crying the whole time. This was the price I had to pay for emancipation, so I just accepted it. I couldn't wait to leave.

Some years, she would come to the bus to see me off wearing huge Jackie O sunglasses to hide her red and swollen eyes. Other years, she didn't come at all, and my father took me to the bus. She could never bring herself to hug me or wish me a good summer.

The JCs go up to camp a few days after the senior counsellors ("SCs"). There was a time-honoured tradition that the male SCs greeted the JC bus to scope out the new crop of female staff. It was very important to look cute getting off that bus. Of course, the girls were sussing out the boys as much as they were us.

I ended up dating an SC—extra points for dating a guy a year older. The nights I was on duty in my unit, he would sit with me. After one of his days off, he returned with a box of Laura Secord miniature lollipops as a gift. It was a sweet, innocent, and short-lived romance that ran its course after a few weeks.

That summer, I also found "my squad," Laurie, Debbie, and Gilla. They were already close friends, and I became their fourth musketeer. Debbie, Gilla, and I were cute. Laurie was gorgeous. She had a God-given Pamela Anderson body, a natural blonde with striations in her hair that glowed in the sunlight. You knew that if you were with Laurie, no one was looking at you. Forty-seven years later, the four of us are still fiercely devoted to each other. We have weathered the death of parents, marital break-ups, a premature baby, a seriously ill child, and conflicting ideologies, but we always have each other's backs. Some of us also swapped boyfriends back then—the hard and fast girl code rule that you are never supposed to break—but we weathered that too.

We had very little use for the other female counsellors at camp. But we had a lot of time for the male counsellors, frequently executing forbidden late-night excursions. We got very little sleep, but we still mustered the energy to have fun and be great with the campers. I'm sure the other female counsellors thought we were stuck-up mean girls. They weren't wrong.

Camp allows you to adopt a different persona. I was way cooler at camp than I was back in the city, and I revelled in it. I had gone through elementary and high school with the same group of kids. You were labelled early. Cool, nerd, smart, not so smart. Camp was that opportunity I was looking for to reinvent myself and escape those labels. I had two advantages. Boys now liked me, and I was a fearless rule-breaker. Sneaking around with boys after curfew, getting drunk on nights when we were able to leave camp, sharing multiple pitchers of sangria with my friends.

Back in the real world in September, I was starting CEGEP (College of General and Professional Teaching), which was a mandatory two-year program before vocational training or university. This had been instituted by the province of Quebec after it was determined that sixteen and seventeen-year-olds were too young to handle the university experience. I did what most of my friends did and attended a private CEGEP. A lot of the students had come from private girls' and boys' schools and went completely hog-wild in this new co-ed environment.

I was already well down the nightlife path so, for me, this was not the biggest draw. Rather, I saw it as a new feeding ground to find a boyfriend. I assumed the best way to let boys know that you are "open for business" was to dress provocatively. Being preppy was in—our CEGEP was actually a former monastery and some nuns still taught there—but I didn't see how wearing loafers and a button-down shirt was going to attract this much-desired boyfriend. Being very goal-oriented, I decided to kick the sexuality thing into high gear.

On my weekend bar-hopping excursions, I left through the back door of the house, which meant I had to walk through the kitchen where my mother was often sitting at the table reading. My favourite outfit was a green over-dye mini skirt, black opaque tights, four-inch-high black patent leather stiletto pumps, a white tuxedo blouse, and the shawl collar tuxedo jacket my father got married in. The jacket fell to the same length as the mini skirt. I had mastered the "no pants" look decades before it became a thing.

I strutted into the kitchen. My mother glanced up from her book. "Where are you going?" she inquired.

"Out," I said. Give nothing away. She had a disapproving look on her face. Wait for it.

"Why do you have to get your self-esteem from a pair of pants?"

Fair question. I looked at her and calmly replied, "I have to get it from somewhere." I headed out into the night, the satisfying click of the back door lock confirming my escape.

I discovered my sexual currency during this time. Even if I didn't like a boy, I enjoyed the validation that he was attracted to me. It was like a cat and mouse game, but I was still on the prowl.

I met Kevin in the school auditorium the first week of the second semester at CEGEP. We happened to sit next to each other while waiting to make a course change. He was beautiful. Chiselled features, blond curly hair, and an athletic body. He had a girlfriend, so we began hanging out together as friends. Soon, the girlfriend was toast, and I had my first serious boyfriend. I wanted to dispense with my virginity as soon as possible. Kevin had been sleeping with his girlfriend, so he had already had that experience, and he seemed wary of my eagerness. He told me we should wait until I turned eighteen.

Kevin and I planned my romantic deflowering for May 9, one day after my eighteenth birthday. My parents were going out to dinner and then to the symphony. Our military-timed operation began at 6:30 p.m.

We made lasagna from a kit that provided all the ingredients, which we ate so quickly that I got indigestion. Then up to my childhood bedroom, where my neatly organized stuffed animals watched. When it was over, I remember thinking, this is what all the fuss is about? There was some blood on the sheets, but since our cleaning lady did the laundry, there was no danger of my mother discovering the evidence.

Kevin lived in the basement of his parent's house, which offered us a lot of privacy. His mother was extremely lenient and had no problem with us spending hours in the basement with the door closed. That's where I eventually did learn what all the fuss was about.

Kevin's mother was the antithesis of mine. She had four children, cooked individual meals to suit everyone's preferences, taught piano, exercised daily, and rarely lost her cool. We became very close, attending fitness classes together. The more time I spent with her, the angrier I became with my mother. This was what a "normal" mother was like. My mother hardly did anything. She was a good cook but didn't enjoy having to cook for us. Her societal contribution was sitting on a few charitable committees and complaining about the amount of work she had to do. Kevin's mother was, in contrast, a dynamo. She made me realize I wanted to be a dynamo, too. Not a lady of leisure, constantly imparting unwanted wisdom on her daughter.

That year, I got sick right before my parents left on a two-week trip to California. We all assumed I would be fine. When I kept getting worse, my father arranged, from California, for me to take a blood test with the head of hematology at the hospital where he worked. I was informed thirty minutes later that I had mono. When I told my parents, my mother said, "You don't want us to come home, do you?" Well yes, actually, I did. I was really sick. But I told them to stay, that it was manageable.

It was ironic. There were very few times that I really needed my mother, but this was one of them. Despite my aversion to her constant diatribe of warnings and advice, I always believed that if, in fact, I wanted her to be there for me, she would. I could barely get out of bed. I was exhausted but felt too sick to sleep, so I just kept popping Gravol.

When they finally returned, I dragged myself out of bed and waited at the top of the stairs to greet them. My mother took one look at me and burst into tears. I'd dropped to ninety pounds. Maybe she felt guilty for not rushing home. Her reaction annoyed me. She had made her decision, now own it. Was I supposed to feel badly for her that I was so sick?

I was becoming increasingly impatient with my mother. I was also spending most of my time at Kevin's house. The more I stayed away, the angrier she became. I was very vocal about what I thought her shortcomings were. I told her that her reactions and need to control me were not normal. During her tirades, she would shriek at me that it was convenient to have a crazy mother that I could blame everything on. She was wrong. I didn't want to blame anyone; I just wanted to navigate the minefield and come out intact.

The next summer, Kevin and I went to camp together. He did not like it. Too many rules. But I was in my happy place.

In September, we both started at McGill as film majors. For midterms, we needed to write a film analysis paper. Kevin left his to the last minute and asked to see mine. Unbeknownst to me, he "borrowed" significantly from my essay. I was an A-student in that class, so I was very surprised when I got a call from the teaching assistant just before the holiday break that I had to meet with him urgently.

I arrived at the TA's small office with no clue as to why I was there. He didn't waste any time telling me that I would have gotten an A on the paper but since Kevin and I turned in such similar papers, he was failing us both. I was shocked. He was failing me? How could Kevin have done that to me?

I was so panicked that I immediately threw Kevin under the bus and said it was me that had written the paper. The TA said it didn't matter. Then he basically insinuated that if I slept with him, he wouldn't fail me. Not an option I was willing to entertain. I fled his office as quickly as I could. I completed the class but never went to his tutorials again. I lambasted Kevin for putting me in that position.

A few years later, I was at an engagement party in Ottawa, and there was the TA. He left around ten minutes after he saw me. He was there with a woman, maybe his wife, who knows. He didn't speak to me. I should have told him to go fuck himself.

That summer, Kevin and I went back to camp. I guess he felt he would rather spend the summer with me, even if it meant being somewhere he wasn't all that keen about. Midway through the summer, I answered the phone in my unit's rec hall. It was Kevin. He had been fired and had to leave immediately, would I come with him? I was having a hard time figuring out why he was getting kicked out. Eventually, he told me it was because he had been found in a female counsellor's bunk, which was forbidden. He swore it was totally innocent. I highly doubted that. I told him I was not going to quit. I went down to say goodbye, but I stayed for the rest of the summer. We continued dating when I got back to Montreal.

We were still together when I went back to camp the following summer. Kevin obviously did not. We were two and a half years into our relationship at this point. I thought Kevin and I were destined to be together forever. Even though I was only twenty, I was sure we would get married. Enter Michael Romoff, whose presence in my life had been foreshadowed from the time I was twelve.

Michael's older brother Brad was on the camp canoeing staff. Every girl at camp knew who Brad Romoff was. He was incredibly handsome. Blond hair, blue eyes, a Jewish Adonis. Every afternoon, the campers were allowed to choose which activity we wanted to participate in. I, like many of the girls in my unit, chose canoeing.

One afternoon, I was having a chat with a girl who went to school with Brad. She said, and I quote: "If you think Brad is cute, you should see his younger brother Michael."

Fast forward five years to my JC year at camp. My friend Debbie starts dating Stan, who happens to be close friends with Michael, who was not at camp. Michael and I were both single at the time, so Debbie and Stan decided to fix us up. And then Stan reneged. He thought I was too mean. That I would chew up Michael and spit him out.

Three years later, fate intervened. I was twenty, Michael was twenty-two and already at law school in Toronto. He didn't have any summer plans, so at the last minute, he was hired by the camp as a tripper. Trippers are the designated staff members that take campers out on wilderness trips. They are usually outdoor enthusiasts. Michael was not. Nor was he a good swimmer or able to read a map. Because he was older, he was allowed to live in "the village," which had fewer rules and no curfew. I was also a staff member in the village.

I distinctly remember our first meeting. Michael was sitting on the stairs of the rec hall with one of the unit heads. My first thought? Very cute!

We became fast friends. Michael had his own tent high up on a hill that was isolated from the other tents. I spent hours up there with him talking late into the night. There was clearly an attraction between us, but I had a boyfriend which I was very clear about.

The village was a quarter mile walk from main camp through the woods. One night when we were walking back together, I stumbled, and he grabbed me around the waist, so I didn't fall. I felt a surge of electricity run through me. Uh oh.

My unit was heading out on a seven-day canoe trip. Michael was assigned as my tripper. I was the only staff member. Fate.

Staff slept in the same tent while the campers were in separate tents. On that first night, we had "the talk." We obviously liked each other but taking our relationship to the next level was complicated. I had a boyfriend I cared about deeply. Michael lived in Toronto. But with the loons singing their mournful song, the inevitable happened.

We had an agreement. A summer fling. That would be the extent of it. On the last day of the canoe trip, when we arrived at the pickup point where the bus would retrieve us the next day, there was a hamburger stand. Camp rules delineated that we were not allowed to purchase food, but Michael and I were both rule breakers and treated our campers to a feast. While we sat on picnic tables gobbling down cheeseburgers and fries, a limousine pulled up to the stand. We were in the middle of nowhere. Then a bride and groom got out. *Hmmmmmm.*

Camp ended. Michael and I said goodbye in the parking lot where we were dropped off. We lasted about five hours before he called me. I broke up with Kevin. I still feel pangs of guilt about it. Michael and I became official.

In many ways, Kevin and I were a good couple. We were crazy about each other, but monogamy was not our strong suit. I think that we were both insecure, and attention from the opposite sex proved to be too intoxicating.

At the time, my relationship with my mother was deteriorating significantly. We were constantly at each other, arguing about everything. I tried to be out of the house as much as possible to avoid conflict.

I wanted out from under my mother's thumb. I was done with the endless unsolicited advice, the criticism, the screaming when I wouldn't accede to her wishes. I was now an adult and wanted to make my own decisions, and she was not ready to let that happen. This is one of the central tragedies of our relationship. She so much wanted to be an integral part of my life. And truthfully, I wanted that too. But not on her terms. I had fought so hard to sever the steel cables of her apron strings that I could not allow her back in.

She was the single most difficult thing in my life. This woman, who I knew loved me but couldn't modify her behaviour to interact with her now adult child. So, I mentally excised her. She was just background noise.

Things had gotten so bad between us that my father agreed that I could move out with Debbie in the fall, and that he would foot the bill. Debbie's brother lived in lower Westmount and had an apartment for rent. It was a five-minute drive from my parents' house. I couldn't wait to move out. My mother was resigned to the idea. The current living situation was untenable for everyone.

I began travelling to Toronto every other weekend to visit Michael while juggling full-time studies at McGill. Then one day, it occurred to me that if I transferred universities, I could get away from my mother AND be with Michael. I went behind my parents' backs and applied to York University in Toronto. I received the acceptance in November and informed my parents that I would be moving on January 1. This set in motion a three-year odyssey of my mother's unrelenting fury.

It took me a while to find an apartment in Toronto so, at first, I stayed with Michael and his younger brother Earl in the university's graduate residence. I eventually rented a nice one-bedroom apartment a short walk from campus.

A large field separated my apartment from Michael's. Occasionally, I would traverse the field by myself in the middle of the night despite the university's warnings that there was a rapist targeting women in the area. Freedom made me fearless to the point of stupidity.

My parents drove down with a carload of my stuff once I moved. I knew my father would have been bearing the brunt of my mother's attacks after I left. Plus, he was still supporting me financially, so she held him responsible for my escape. It had to have been awful for him at home.

Not surprisingly, things were combative from the moment I opened the door. My mother and I were constantly bickering, and my father was beginning to lose patience with me. Things escalated, I was yelling and swearing at my mother. Completely exasperated, my father slapped me across the face and split my lip.

With blood trickling down my chin, I shrieked at the top of my lungs for them to get the fuck out, which they did. What haunts me to this day is not that my father hit me, but how horribly he must have felt about it. I didn't hold my father responsible; I blamed it on my mother.

For public consumption, my mother would tell anyone she came in contact with that the problem was not that I left, but that I had done it in the middle of a school year. "Who does that?" was her constant refrain. The truth was, she just couldn't let me go. She was not done "mothering" me. It was all she focused on. She spoke to her friends about it. She spoke to MY friends about it when they would come over to visit whenever I was back in Montreal. It made everyone feel very uncomfortable and I hated going home. All she did was rant at me. She was completely consumed by what she perceived as me abandoning her.

My mother sucked up all the air. My anxiety over moving out on my own, living in a new city, and starting this chapter of my life didn't matter. My father's sadness that his daughter had left home didn't matter. Only HER feelings were important.

Separation was one of my mother's greatest fears and, by moving to Toronto to be with Michael, I had made that fear a reality. Intellectually, I understood that her anger was just an expression of her feeling rejected, but that is cold comfort when the anger is directed at you.

Her endless diatribes were like a video loop on repeat, saying the same things over and over again, with absolutely no interest in anyone's response. No one could manage her out-of-proportion reaction.

During our many conversations about how we could have a better relationship, I literally begged her to stop micromanaging me. Her constant stream of unsolicited advice and criticism was unappreciated and was only harming our relationship. Her response was that as my mother, it was her duty to point out all the things she thought I was doing wrong, and there were a lot of them.

It was a rash decision to switch schools in the middle of the year. I was too young and irresponsible to live on my own. How could I just give up everything for a boy? It was costing them a fortune to support me.

One of the first things I did when I moved to Toronto was cut my hair. I went to a new stylist and asked for a shag cut. I emerged with something more akin to a mullet. It wasn't great, but it grew out into a Boy George-ish, multi-layered look that I really liked. If a piece was out of place, I'd just chop it off myself. Easy peasy. I knew my mother would be appalled at my DIY styling, but she was 336 miles away in Montreal. I didn't have to worry about it in the short term.

A few months after I moved to Toronto, my cousin Charlotte got married in Montreal. At the out-of-towners dinner the night before the wedding, I was seated directly across from my mother at a long, beautifully set table. Ironically, it was at La Diligence, the same venue as my sweet sixteen. She kept staring at me. *Appetizer.* I could feel her eyes boring into me. *First course.* The stare! *Someone made a toast.* Seriously, her stare was like an ER doctor's flashlight in the face of a car crash victim. Finally, she announced loudly, "I can't bear to look at you."

The table went completely silent. I got up, shaking, found my way to the bathroom and promptly burst into tears. Charlotte's sister Sandi coaxed me back to the table.

My father had had enough. He insisted that my mother see a psychiatrist. She agreed to three sessions. I don't know what happened in the first, but it must have been significant because my father called to tell me the psychiatrist wanted me to attend the second session with my mother. His tone was calm but firm. This wasn't a request, it was nonnegotiable. And the appointment was the following week, so, I flew to Montreal as instructed.

There we were, my mother and I, sitting side by side on a cheap brown couch in the psychiatrist's office. I had never been to a therapy session. I had no idea know what to expect. What had my mother disclosed to the therapist in the first appointment that made it so crucial I be there for the second?

My mother, who appeared to be quite composed, did most of the talking. She had been going on about these issues for months, so she was well-practiced in her eloquent delivery. The common complaints: "How unacceptable it was for me to change schools in the middle of the year. I was ruining my life and hers. I was too young and irresponsible to be living on my own." She showed none of the hysteria that accompanied those messages when they were angrily flung at me in the middle of the night. I sat there and took it in. What was I supposed to say? My mother is profoundly overprotective and refuses to let me grow up?

It took the psychiatrist exactly thirty minutes to share his viewpoint.

Pointing at me. "You are the adult."

Pointing at her. "You are the child."

My mother scoffed. "That's ridiculous, I'm her mother." While she continued to object, I sat there stunned, trying to make sense of this Freaky Friday observation. It all fit. A parent is supposed to meet a child's needs, but I was expected to meet my mother's.

Despite my mother's bluster, I could tell the words stung. I think the psychiatrist was incredibly irresponsible springing that on my mother before he understood how it could affect her. She did the third session on her own, and that was it. She never went back.

By leaving Montreal, I firmly put my needs ahead of hers. Having a difficult mother was something I had grown up with. This new phase was just an escalation of the relationship we had always had. I had no room for empathy for my mother.

Meanwhile, back in Toronto, I was having a pretty great time. I was pursuing an Honours degree in English Literature, and I got my first job waitressing at Kelly's. Kelly's was a huge, busy restaurant and bar at Ontario Place, a summer attraction on the shore of Lake Ontario. I had no waitressing experience, so I sort of fudged that I had worked at Gert's, the popular student pub at McGill. I did spend a lot of time there, but it had been eating pizza and getting drunk, not serving customers.

The restaurant's uniforms were an affront to my fashion sensibilities. We had to wear kelly-green polo shirts paired with a below-the-knee beige polyester skirt. Hideous! My only option for personal expression was through shoes and accessories.

I bought these adorable black, pointed-toe, kitten heel shoes. Never mind that they became excruciating during a long shift, they were also life endangering. Kelly's had a wood slat patio that was considered the plum section for making money, as people drank a lot out there. My kitten heels were just slightly narrower than the space between the wooden slats. Consequently, they frequently got wedged in between, which would stop me and my tray in our tracks.

In case you didn't know it, pilsner beer glasses are famously "tippy." After numerous incidents involving having to apologize to guests for spilling a tray of beer on them, I relented and bought more sensible shoes.

And then there were the earrings. I wore the biggest, most ridiculous designs I could find. The best ones looked like giant black clams with oversized pearls peeking out at the bottom. And they were heavy—pull-your-earlobes-down heavy—but they definitely made a statement.

Despite my resistance to the uniform, I was a pretty good waitress and I enjoyed the job. There was a very active party atmosphere at the restaurant after hours. It was where I learned to drink scotch neat, as introduced to me by one of the managers I was friendly with. I liked the shock value of it. This little girl who was able to down copious amounts of hard liquor.

When I returned to university that fall, I learned that if I dropped the Honours designation for my degree that I would be able to graduate a year early, which seemed like a great idea. That meant Michael and I would graduate at the same time.

We bade farewell to the desolate university campus and moved into a cute basement apartment next to Grace Church on-the-Hill, which is featured prominently in the book *A Prayer for Owen Meany* by John Irving. I read the book when I was living there. It is my favourite book of all time.

I "failed to mention" my new living arrangement to my parents. Four months after we moved in together, my parents were in town visiting and asked if Michael would be joining us for dinner. Yes, he would. Oh, and by the way, we are now living together. They looked surprised but let it go.

Now, I was intent on building a career. When I was still at university in Montreal, I had zero ambition. My parents would have been fine with me staying in school until I got married, most likely to a doctor, and then staying home to raise kids. I would have also been fine with that. I was unmotivated to do well in university. Then I found myself in Toronto with a degree in English Literature. All my friends were either still in school becoming doctors and lawyers, or working. I hated school, so I did not want to do another degree. My parents were still supporting me monetarily, but obviously I needed to start standing on my own two feet.

I was initially interested in advertising and publishing. I went to see a vocational counsellor. She looked to be in her early fifties, dowdily dressed, librarian glasses. I shared my dreams and aspirations. She informed me that those were very competitive industries, and I did not appear to be special enough to break into them. Yes, she actually said that. I told her I would be willing to start in an administrative capacity, and she responded that if I did, I would never rise through the ranks. I was incensed. After a fifteen-minute conversation, this woman decided I would not succeed. She did not know me. She did not know what I was capable of. She offered no advice whatsoever—not to go back to school for programs that specialize in those areas, not to seek out unpaid internships. Nothing. When I received a form asking for feedback on my experience with the counsellor, I sent back a scathing review.

It was, however, true that I had no real-world work experience. There were always jobs available at headhunting firms, mainly because the remuneration was all commission-based, and it was soul-sucking work that very few people stuck with. So, I answered an ad for one and was hired to work in the "technical" division. This meant I spent my days trying to persuade manufacturing plant managers that my clients had the perfect skillset to join their team of equipment repair technicians. All for the low, low commission of fifteen percent of the potential employee's first year of salary. Clearly, this was not the perfect job for me. I had no knowledge or interest in this industry, but I gave it a shot.

On my first day, I was given a manual and told to go read it in the boardroom. While I was in there, two managers, one of whom I reported to, came in to have a private discussion. They didn't acknowledge my existence, so I just kept reading. They were having a dispute about the commission on a specific file. My manager then said to the other, "Don't Jew me down." I froze. My boss was a vocal antisemite. As far as I knew, he didn't know I was Jewish. But how would he feel about me if he found out? I was not brave enough to confront him, so I went back to reading the manual. Months later, when we had developed a good working relationship, I brought it up and told him how upsetting that was. He was surprised that I was offended. He came from an Irish working-class background. He didn't realize how it would land. To him, it was just "an expression."

We worked in a shared open space with our desks set up in "quads." Four of us sat facing each other. We had big hardcover directories, divided by industry, that were considered our bibles. We sat there from 9 a.m. to 5 p.m., minus a lunch break, cold-calling employers. In those days, you could smoke at your desk. So, I did. A lot. It must have been brutal for the non-smokers in the office. I smoked, I drank coffee, and I talked on the phone. When you closed a deal, you rang a bell in the office. This was decades before *Selling Sunset* made that kind of bell ring famous. And then you got to go into the prize closet and choose something like a water filter or a set of glasses. I hated every minute of that job but, much to my surprise, I was very good at it and began making placements.

You weren't allowed to take any vacation days until you had been there for a year. Michael's family was going to Florida, and we had been invited to join them. I was months away from vacation days. So, I quit. As per company protocol, you immediately had to leave the office. This was on a Friday. Monday morning, I received a call from one of the other division heads asking if I would consider coming back and working for her. No thank you.

This became a pattern. If I didn't like a job, I would start looking for another one. One year, I had four T4s (the year-end tax document that each employer sends you). My friends told me I was crazy. That prospective employers would think that I was flighty. It actually never was an issue.

I responded to an ad for a coordinator position at a large property management company. My time would be split between assisting the marketing director and a property manager. It was a mixed-use property in the heart of downtown that included a ninety-store retail mall and a forty-storey office tower. This sounded more my speed. I interviewed and got the job. I was paid a paltry $12,000 a year—which was less than I spent annually on clothes and shoes.

With daddy's credit card in hand, I put together a business wardrobe. Linen suits for the summer, tweed dresses for the winter, and a selection of pumps. I also bought a briefcase. I had nothing to put in my briefcase, but I dreamed of the day I would need it to bring home work because I was too busy to get it all done during the day.

For the marketing director, I helped plan events for the shopping concourse and sold ads for a promo coupon booklet featuring special offers from the stores. For the property manager, I collected rent and compiled retail sales figures.

From the moment I started what I considered "my first big girl job," I realized that I had ambition. I had inherited my father's work ethic. I was the first one in the office in the morning and the last to leave. The administrative part of the job was boring, so I devised a way to keep myself motivated. Three days at the beginning of each month were allocated to collecting sales figures from the retailers. By my third month on the job, I was doing it in two. I also sold more ads in that promo coupon book than anyone else ever had.

The constant refrain at my parent-teacher interviews when I was in high school was that "Audrey isn't living up to her potential." I should have been getting better grades, but it just wasn't one of my priorities. I also didn't understand how they knew what my potential was. But now it all made sense to me. In the working world, I finally felt like I was seen. People thought that I was smart and capable. I wanted to do well. I wanted to get promoted. My self-esteem shifted from social acceptance to corporate success. A new chapter in self-discovery.

My competence was being noticed by the higher-ups, and the marketing director didn't like it. She was tiny in stature but a bit of a tyrant. She told me that I had to take my lunch hour when she did, so that I was always available in case she needed me. It was ridiculous. She had serious delusions of grandeur.

The property was located at a very busy intersection with a lot of foot traffic, so the marketing director came up with the idea of hosting fashion shows outside on the stairs of the property. Cool—*fashion!* This was something I was passionate about. Unfortunately, she also decided I would be the perfect candidate to sell event T-shirts from a cart on the sidewalk. She insisted I wear the event T-shirt. Nobody puts baby in the corner . . . and nobody dictates what Audrey wears. To foil her evil intent, I wore dresses on the days I was supposed to be manning the cart. I couldn't possibly wear the T-shirts because I had no skirt or pants to match with them.

There were big conferences in the retail industry run by the International Council of Shopping Centers (ICSC). The marketing director always attended. Opening her mail was one of my duties, and I became alerted to an upcoming conference. I left the information on her desk with a post-it note saying that I would also like to attend. The next day, I was in her office when she wasn't there, and I noticed the post-it was in the garbage. *Hell no!*

I brought the conference attendance information to the property manager and asked if I could attend. He readily agreed. He was her boss too, so she was powerless to stop me. At the conference, I discovered a group of fabulous women who worked as marketing directors in powerhouse malls. That's what I wanted to be too.

Between the marketing director's concerted efforts to not include me in important meetings and my acts of civil disobedience, it was clear that I had to move on. I started looking for another job. I was offered, and accepted, a marketing manager position at a different shopping complex. Eight months after I left, I received a call from the property manager at my previous job. The former marketing director had been fired, and they were hoping I would come back and replace her. It wasn't that I hated my current job—my boss was a very nice man—but I suspected he might have a drinking problem. He would frequently take the management team out for boozy lunches, which he charged to his corporate expense account. This was the 1980s. This was standard operating procedure. My liver and I jointly decided that it was probably a good idea to return to my former employer.

I was happy at the new job for two years before I got bored. The adult iteration of "the better carrot." People kept telling me I should go into public relations. I had no idea what that was. My shopping complex had teamed up with three other downtown centres to run a charitable holiday gift-wrapping program. The woman who put the program together was the PR person for one of the other malls. We worked together closely, and I decided I wanted to work for her. It was just a small boutique agency, but I let her know if there was ever an opening, I would be interested.

I had another reason for wanting to work for her. Her agency handled the PR for a huge trade and consumer show called "The Festival of Canadian Fashion." This was a very big deal. The fashion shows attracted upward of ten thousand people and the media sponsor was FashionTelevision (FT). FT was the genius creation of Citytv, a Toronto-based, scrappy, innovative broadcaster. FT travelled the world covering fashion weeks and designers. It had become a huge global hit. I was obsessed with it and with its host Jeanne Beker. I felt that fashion PR would be the perfect job for me. A few months later, the call came from the agency. There was an opening.

The thing about PR is it looks really glamourous from the outside. High-profile celebrities, world-famous designers, and flashy events. It is also high stress and long hours. But I didn't care. I *loved* it. One of the advantages of working at a small agency is you get to work on every aspect of the business. Before long, I was handling clients and planning fashions shows.

There were only three of us at the agency: my boss, me, and a junior, Deborah McNamara, who started a week before me. She was very nice and very smart, but I was initially not a fan. She came in late every morning. We were supposed to be there at 9 a.m. I was always early. She'd come flying in at 9:15 every day with the excuse that the bus was running late. I was annoyed. I felt that she didn't take initiative. She didn't seem to know anything about the job.

A few months later, my boss called me into her office and told me she wanted to do a performance review for Deborah and requested my input. I let loose about what I perceived to be all of Deborah's shortcomings. When the boss called Deborah into her office to do the review, she told her that I was unhappy with her. How do I know this? Because Deborah did something incredible.

Once our boss left for the day, she knocked on the door of my office and asked if we could talk. She told me what the boss had said in her review. She was very calm and genuinely wanted to know how she could improve. I was not happy that my boss had thrown me under the bus, but I was incredibly impressed with how Deborah handled the situation. I knew I could sometimes be intimidating, and she still walked into the lion's den to deal with the issue head on. She was not defensive; she did not make excuses. My opinion of her changed completely. I also learned that this was her first job, while our boss had positioned her to me as experienced. I became Deborah's mentor and champion. She was the first employee I hired when I started my own agency. Deborah now runs her own successful publishing company. Thirty-five years later, we still share a deep bond.

The Royal Wedding Debacle

I WAS ON A SUCCESSFUL CAREER PATH and now I wanted to tick the marriage box. When Michael and I hit the five-year mark of coupledom, I started aggressively pursuing my objective. The bridesmaid dresses in my closet were accumulating and I was feeling very insecure about being the only one in my tight-knit friend group that was going to be left behind.

One day when I was visiting my parents in Montreal while Michael stayed in Toronto, I asked him again, over the phone, "When are we going to get married?" This time his response was, "When do you want to?" Hold on. He had never said that before! It was always "not yet." The door had cracked open, and I was going to bust through it.

"Does that mean we are engaged?" I asked. He responded yes, but that if I told anyone about it, the engagement would be off. I think he was only half kidding. No rose petals strewn about the room, no bent knee. There I was in Montreal, newly engaged, and not allowed to tell anyone.

When Michael and I spoke later that day, he revealed that he had already begun telling his friends that we were engaged. We were official! I flew downstairs to tell my parents, who were thrilled. Especially my mother.

She immediately sprung into action. Within forty-eight hours, we had a date, a venue, a caterer, two bands, a photographer, and a videographer. When it was important to her, she could hustle. Since the wedding was going to be in Montreal, and I knew that she would turn it into a showcase for herself, I was fine trusting her with the details. She, however, took this to mean that I was not allowed to have any input.

On a trip to New York, my mother picked up a Van Cleef & Arpels catalogue to look at ring designs. She had a few loose diamonds and had generously offered that I could choose one for my ring. I knew exactly which one I wanted . . . it had been smuggled out of Europe in my grandmother's best friend's tooth. It wasn't huge and it was chipped, but that diamond symbolized triumph over great adversity, and I loved that. My mother and I designed the ring together, a diamond bezel setting with two rows of channel-set rubies. My mother's jewellery designer created the ring.

I never asked when the ring would be ready. I just assumed that she would let me know. Later, on another trip to Montreal, Michael's father picked us up at the airport. Michael got into the back seat with me which I though was weird. On the drive, Michael pulled out the ring. He and my mother had colluded to surprise me. Kudos on the surprise portion, less so on the ambiance. But I was thrilled to finally be wearing an engagement ring.

And then the battles with my mother began. Over my china pattern, over the wedding menu, and unsurprisingly, over THE DRESS.

I did the initial dress recon on my own and then my mother came to Toronto to see what I'd chosen. She didn't like the dress I selected. It had a big poofy overlay around the waist, which she said I was too short to pull off, and she claimed it was too expensive. I knew that was bullshit. She would have spent anything on a dress she liked. It was clear that this one didn't fit her vision for me.

Back to the drawing board. I did a second shopping mission in Toronto. This time, I was sure I had found the perfect dress. It was very fitted, hugged my slim silhouette, and was covered in sequins and seed pearls like something Bob Mackie would have designed for Cher. And it was much less expensive than the last one.

The wedding dress boutique had a carpeted pedestal surrounded on three sides by mirrors to amplify the drama of the moment. I stepped out of the dressing room onto the pedestal, excitedly taking my place where thousands of brides had stood before me. My mother was seated on a poofy sofa. I was beaming as I anticipated the rush of emotion. She took a moment and then said, "You look like a concentration camp survivor." Whump. A verbal gut punch. Her implication, I looked too skinny. That was one of the cruelest things she had ever said to me. That comment abruptly ended our shopping excursion. She left for Montreal the following day. I wasn't speaking to her.

Like she so often did, my mother wore me down. I realized it was going to be easier to just get the wedding dress in Montreal where she could essentially choose what she wanted me to wear. Eventually, we found a gown that was the epitome of 1980s overstatement. Italian lace, puffy sleeves, hundreds of buttons down the back, an exaggerated peplum, and of course, a royal length train. The dress had been discontinued, probably because it was so over the top that no other bride would dare to wear it.

My mother and I both loved the dress, but the whole dress-shopping experience was extremely painful for me otherwise. I never learned to temper my expectations for my mother's behaviour. I clung, instead, to a fantasy that this time it would be different, but it never was.

My mother had a unique ability to disabuse herself of the chaos she created. Once she calmed down, however long that took, she was fine, acknowledging that it had been rough period, but all was good now, wasn't it? Except, I was not good. I felt like a vase that kept getting smashed and glued back together. Eventually, the pieces just didn't fit anymore.

A few months later, my mother unveiled her own dress. A form-fitting, light blue, sequined dress that Bob Mackie would have designed for Cher. I'm sure she never even realized how similar it was to the "concentration camp" wedding dress.

I was also allowed no say over the wedding invitations. I went to Montreal to go over wedding details and found out that my mother had already ordered them. That turned out to be a huge mistake. The copy laid out my parents' names first, then mine, followed by Michael's and his parents. Truthfully, that was perfectly acceptable protocol, but Michael's parents freaked out. They thought it looked like they were second-class citizens. Now, Michael and his parents were mad at me.

I was extremely angry with my mother. Not so much about the wording, but because it was inconceivable to me that I had no say in my own wedding invitation. Somehow, my father got dragged into the fray and my mother became furious with him. The day I left Montreal, things were still simmering. When I spoke to my dad that night, he informed me that my mother was leaving him and that she said it was my fault. It was always my fault, or my father's. This was her MO. It was not the first time she threatened to leave my father. She never did it. The closest she came was leaving the house and walking around the block, but the threat of it was always deeply unsettling.

My mother was out of town when I went to Montreal to select my china pattern, so I went shopping with my aunt Ruthie and my cousin Sandi. I was very excited about choosing my pattern. Another bridal rite of passage I had been anticipating for years. There were hundreds of options to choose from. We chose a black, white, and pink floral pattern—we all thought it was very pretty. When I took my mother to the store a few weeks later to show it to her, she was horrified. It was not a particularly "good" brand, and she thought her friends would find it tacky. An all-out screaming match ensued in the middle of the store, with people staring at us and our poor sales associate at a loss as how to handle the situation.

Finally, I yelled at her, "Why don't you just choose it then?" I was being sarcastic, but she took it seriously. How it reflected on HER was more important than me liking my dishes. She chose a Royal Crown Derby orange, white, and gold cloisonné pattern. They were actually quite beautiful, and expensive, but the experience was so negative that they stayed sealed in the shipping box for fourteen years before I even opened them. Thirty-five years later, I have barely used them.

My mother had given up smoking in her thirties, but she occasionally bummed cigarettes from Michael, who was a smoker. During one of their clandestine smoking sessions a few months before the wedding, she told Michael that she would understand if he didn't want to marry me. She didn't provide any reasons. Maybe it was because she and I were fighting so much. Maybe she thought that if Michael and I broke up, I would move back to Montreal.

Whatever her reason, Michael didn't tell me until after we were married. I never confronted my mother about it. Obviously, I was hurt. It was a horrible thing to say. Did she think I was so awful that Michael should consider leaving me? Maybe she was just trying to be funny? Michael and I certainly didn't laugh about it.

July 2, 1989 . . . my wedding day. At 9 a.m., my mother, Naomi (my matron of honour), and I headed off to the hairdresser my mother booked. Immediately, Naomi and I knew something was off. The stylist was either coked up or hungover from the night before. He still did a decent job creating my half up, half down hairstyle. We didn't say anything about his state to my mother, but she picked up on it and was very unimpressed, repeatedly expressing to us how unprofessional it was.

The entire day felt like an endurance test. Get up early, get your hair done, go home, grab the dress, the jewellery, and the two pairs of shoes (the high-heeled version and the lower-heeled version that you change into when your feet start to hurt). Then off to the synagogue. Get dressed. Take pictures. It was a scorching hot day, and I was very concerned that my hair would frizz.

The wedding party included eleven bridesmaids and eleven ushers. Many members of the wedding party were from out of town and had missed the rehearsal a few days earlier, so I organized a quick run-through that afternoon, just hours before the ceremony. There is video footage of me with my hair and makeup done, dressed in a casual black jumpsuit, holding a clipboard, and telling everyone what to do and where to stand.

While I found the whole event exhausting, my mother was in her element. I had asked her before the wedding how many guests were invited, and was told, "Don't ask." I assumed around three hundred. There were, in fact, four hundred. There is a picture of the ceremony, taken from the balcony, that makes it look like a royal wedding.

What mattered most to me was my speech. At that time, many brides did not speak at their weddings, but I had something to say. It was not about my gratitude to my parents or my undying love for Michael, although both were mentioned. It was about Bubby. This remarkable, resilient woman who had suffered indescribable horrors and remained strong and kind. Who saved herself and my mother. Who built a new life from nothing. Who was now sitting in a ballroom at her granddaughter's wedding. An unfathomable journey from Auschwitz to here.

The wedding was a triumph for my mother as well. Despite the behind-the-scenes drama, the wedding itself was beautiful. She was so happy and proud of herself. She repeatedly said that it was the best wedding she had ever been to.

Life was relatively calm after that. We returned from our honeymoon in California. We went back to work. My parents and grandmother gifted us a down payment on a house, so we bought one in the west end of the city. My mother and I were doing okay. She seemed to have come to terms with the fact that I was building a life in Toronto. Or so I thought.

The Bullshit Myth of Having It All

Ladies and gentlemen, welcome to the Audrey Hyams Romoff three-ring circus! Watch as she juggles persistent morning sickness, newborns, and building a business.

EVENTUALLY, I REALIZED THAT I WAS WORKING A LOT harder than the boss. I was handling everything, writing the pitches, and bringing in new clients. I was also training and managing Deborah. It dawned on me that I would be better off running my own agency. Deborah left to go back to school to finish her degree, and I gave in my notice and started making plans.

I would be working from home and had no employees at that point, so it seemed reasonably risk-free. But what to name this new venture? Most PR agencies incorporate the founders' names, but I had loftier ambitions. I wanted to build a brand.

I initially wanted to call the agency Barracuda Communications because that's what I planned to be. This was met with universal disdain by my sounding boards. Too aggressive.

It was 1990 and the economy was tanking. Michael suggested a name: OverCat. The rationale was that despite the economic headwinds, I would be an "OverCat," not an "underdog." In pitches, potential clients often asked about the origin of the name. When I explained it, they found it amusing. It was also a selling point. If the company had such a clever name, I must be clever too.

I landed my first big client before I formally announced the opening of the agency. I had a close relationship with the marketing director of Yorkdale Shopping Centre, one of North America's biggest and most profitable shopping malls. I took her to lunch to let her know I was leaving. Unbelievably, she told me that she was changing jobs too, moving to a smaller, high-end shopping centre downtown. She offered me the account on the spot. I was twenty-seven years old.

A few months after I started OverCat, Michael and I decided to have a baby. At no point did it ever occur to me that this was going to be problematic. Why would it be? The business was taking off, so I leased space in Michael's office and hired Deborah, who had just completed her degree in journalism.

Michael and I were already booked to go to Aruba to celebrate our second wedding anniversary that July. I was seven weeks pregnant. My morning sickness started a few days before the trip. Michael wanted to cancel but I reassured him everything would be fine. We had an early morning flight and got to the airport at 6 a.m. I could not find the check-in counter. After tearing around the airport, I discovered our flight was the next day. I had completely fucked up the date. Once again, Michael thought we should cancel the trip. And once again, I said it would be fine. I should have listened to Michael . . . it was a disaster.

I was nauseous and miserable for the entire flight. When we arrived at the resort, Michael was starving but I felt too sick to eat. Michael insisted I had to eat something. We went to one of the restaurants in the hotel where you cooked your own meat on a burning hot stone, and I ordered chicken. I had yet to learn that chicken is one of the foods that many pregnant women find revolting. The smell of the chicken cooking on the stone was too much for me. I fled back to the hotel room where I stayed for the entire week, ordering room service and watching the movie channel. Thankfully, there was a casino, so Michael's vacation wasn't completely ruined.

I waited the requisite three months to tell my family. I was terrified of miscarrying in the first trimester. The first call I made was to my grandmother. I was bursting with excitement to tell her, and she was overjoyed. This was the greatest gift I could give her. She had transcended unimaginable horror, was the most incredible grandmother to me, and would now soon be a great-grandmother.

Then, I called my mother. I shared my news. Dead silence on the other end of the line. There was no congratulations. No asking how I was feeling. She immediately launched into a lecture about how irresponsible it was of me to go to Aruba when I was pregnant. "What if something had happened?" which in Rachel-speak, meant I was taking risks that she would not be able to deal with the consequences of. If my mother crumbled when she had her own children, grandchildren meant next-level terror.

She must have realized that, at some point, I was going to get pregnant—I was very vocal about wanting children. I think she wasn't ready. Just like she wasn't ready for me to grow up and leave home.

I was hurt by her reaction. My father was thrilled, but my mother's response stung.

I was working crazy long hours. I had not counted on the full-day morning sickness that lasted throughout my entire pregnancy. It was debilitating. Trying to schedule client meetings during the few moments of the day when I wasn't nauseous was an impossible juggling act. I had to stop doing client breakfasts, lunches, and dinners, because I was always worried that I would throw up. I was terrified that I would lose ground in my career. I hid how sick I was from my clients. I did what was expected of me. What I expected of myself. Clients can be understanding up to a point, but at the end of the day, they still want their money's worth, and you are a commodity.

Working in the fashion industry and wearing shapeless maternity dresses with Peter Pan collars, which was pretty much all that was available at the time, was not going to cut it. I had a seamstress custom-make a maternity wardrobe for me, including a black leather mini skirt and a purple crushed velvet maxi skirt. I had a huge collection of tights and leggings that I wore with cute A-line mini dresses.

My mother never failed to tell me how difficult my pregnancy was on her. She was a nervous wreck. I can certainly understand that feeling. I'm sure I would be very anxious if my daughter was pregnant too, but I would not complain about it to her. There was no room for my own anxiety. I was so tired when I got home from work, the last thing I wanted to do was get on the phone with my mother. She was furious with me for not wanting to spend time reassuring her that I was fine.

The pregnancy bible at the time was *What to Expect When You're Expecting* by Heidi Murkoff. I couldn't wait to buy it. An honour to join the ranks of pregnant women. On one of my trips to Montreal while pregnant, I noticed that my mother had purchased the book as well. For HERSELF.

I literally hated eating. Everything made me nauseous. I was living on a steady diet of greasy Chinese food and Häagen-Dazs ice cream bars. Chocolate mousse was my favourite main course at lunch. I couldn't even take the iron pills that my doctor had recommended because they gave me such bad heartburn. Before I became pregnant, I loved rare roast beef, so I bought some to see if I could tolerate it. I opened the fridge and just looking at it made me throw up. I stopped eating meat, became anemic, and was completely exhausted all the time. I eventually discovered that I could eat breaded shrimp balls and vegetarian lo mein, which I ordered every night from a horrible restaurant called Mr. Pong—mercifully now out of business.

Surprisingly, given my body image issues, I wasn't freaked out about gaining weight. Because I was so nauseous all the time and food didn't appeal to me, I only put on twenty-two pounds, but I loved watching my changing body. I was way more nervous about how this little human was going to make its way out of my body than I was about my expanding shape.

One of our clients was The Hospital for Sick Children Foundation. The hospital is a world-class facility and saves many children's lives. Lindsay and Alex were both treated there for relatively minor issues when they were young. It is a place where miracles happen, but every time I went there for a meeting, I could feel the sorrow leaking from every brick. There was a central atrium at the hospital that you had to walk through to get to the foundation office. The second I walked through those sliding doors into the atrium, the tears started flowing. Small children who lost their hair due to chemotherapy. Children in wheelchairs attached to medical devices. Brave parents whose hearts must have been breaking. Luckily, Deborah also had a relationship with the client, so she took over the meetings. I just couldn't handle being there.

Most of the fashion PR agency owners and fashion magazine editor-in-chiefs were women. I was one of very few who had children. I wondered if prospective clients, both male and female, would worry that I would be less effective because of my familial responsibilities.

When I was seven months pregnant, I had a meeting with the marketing director of a large, national retail chain that had been a client with my previous agency and jumped ship when I started my own. I thought it was just a typical meeting, but when I sat down, she let me know that they were terminating my contract and bringing their business in house. Okay, this wasn't great news, but it did happen from time to time. But the kicker was, then she said to me, "You aren't planning to keep working after you have the baby, are you?"

This woman had two kids herself, and she had returned to work after each maternity leave. I was stunned. I felt it was such a betrayal coming from another woman. I was polite, wished her all the best, and left the office. I was already worried about running a company and having kids. This incident just reinforced my fears.

One afternoon, two weeks before my due date, I was at the office and not feeling well. I poked my head into Michael's office, told him I was having back pain, and asked him to take me home. The office was close to the hospital, but our house was not, so he insisted we go to the hospital first. I told him there was no way I was in labour. This was a first baby, and they are usually late. Deborah informed us that she had been timing my back pains, and they were pretty evenly spaced.

Off we went to the OB-GYN's office at Mount Sinai without an appointment. I apologized for just showing up and assured them I was not in labour. After a quick exam, they assured me that I was, in fact, in labour. Oops. Turns out, you can have back labour.

This was not going according to plan. I was supposed to give a lecture the next day to a class of college students in a public relations program. I didn't want to renege on my commitment. Deborah had been asking me for weeks to share notes with her "just in case," but I had no intention of going into labour before that class. I had Deborah come to the hospital so that I could brief her in between contractions, which I did.

As a result of going straight to the hospital from the office, I didn't have my "pregnancy go bag." In prenatal class, they emphasized that you should have socks because your feet would be cold during delivery. I asked Deborah to buy some and bring them with her to the hospital. In her naïve panic, she chose red—not a colour of sock I ever wore—because she thought they would hide the blood splatters. The socks, however, were not necessary. After the epidural and morphine, I didn't even know that I had feet.

Because Deborah had left the office in the middle of the afternoon, she called our answering service to check messages. A potential client had called inquiring about OverCat's services. When Deborah told me, I did what any responsible business owner would do . . . I called the client back. From the DELIVERY ROOM. They asked if I could come in the following day to meet with them. "Ummmm, no, tomorrow is tough for me," I said, and booked the meeting for four days later. Four days felt, to me, like a long time to leave a prospective client waiting.

Lindsay was a "drama queen" from the start. I pushed for almost three hours. Nothing. Finally, they used a vacuum to deliver her. Apparently, you get very swollen pushing for that long, so when I delivered, everything ripped.

They whisked her away to do whatever they had to do while I was getting stitched up. In the meantime, Michael told me that he was exhausted and wanted to go home and get some sleep. Everything seemed under control. He left and they wheeled me into recovery. I was euphoric. I had a beautiful baby girl. The recovery room was a huge space divided by curtains between the beds. I appeared to be the only one in there. A doctor poked his head in. He informed me that Lindsay was making a grunting noise. Okay. Then he calmly told me that this could indicate respiratory issues including pneumonia. They wanted to run tests and potentially intubate her. He told me he would be back as soon as he could with an update.

I broke down sobbing so loudly that the sound echoed down the hall. There was no phone. I couldn't call Michael. Or Naomi. So I prayed. Begging God to let her be okay. About an hour later, the doctor returned and told me they had ruled out pneumonia but wanted to keep her in the Level 2 special care nursery for observation.

After a few hours, Lindsay was given the all-clear and brought to my room. I have never been more grateful. I decided early in the pregnancy that I was not going to breastfeed. Because I ran my own company, I had to get back to work quickly—which I did, full-time, when she was five weeks old. I also knew that I was not one of those women who would feel comfortable breastfeeding in public.

The nurse who brought Lindsay to me asked if I wanted to try breastfeeding her. I told her that Lindsay would be formula-fed.

She was not impressed. First, she lectured me about the benefits of breastfeeding. I told her I knew, but my preference was to bottle-feed. I think she realized that she was not going to win the battle and begrudgingly told me where to find the bottles of pre-mixed formula. In her eyes, I had clearly failed my first motherhood exam. Throughout the day, a progression of doctors and nurses came to check on us. The first question was always, "How is the breastfeeding going?" Each time, I politely explained that she would be bottle-fed. I eventually became annoyed with their judgemental looks so when the next doctor came in and asked the same question, I told him I would strike a deal. Don't ask me how the breastfeeding is going, and I won't ask you when you last had sex.

Lindsay was born in the middle of the night, but I waited until 6:30 a.m. to call my parents. They told me they would be there later that day and took the train with my grandmother. It was very important to me that my grandmother be there.

They arrived late in the afternoon. Michael must have picked them up at the train station and brought them to the hospital. I don't remember that detail. I just remember all of us, in my private room, experiencing a miracle. With the arrival of this perfect five-pound, eleven-ounce little girl, our family now spanned four generations.

As was standard in those days, you stayed in the hospital for forty-eight hours. After that, our new family headed home. My parents and my grandmother were staying with us. I had this idealized version of all five of us sharing the load of taking care of the baby. My mother had, after all, been a nurse. I assumed she would be helpful navigating a newborn. Instead, we were like the five stooges crashing into each other in our little house. Michael went back to work the day after we got home from the hospital.

My father and grandmother tried to stay out of everyone's way. I was completely overwhelmed. My mother wrought chaos.

The first thing she did was make me completely paranoid about sterilizing the bottles. I had a small supply of pre-filled formula bottles that came home with me from the hospital, but needed to sterilize new bottles and nipples in boiling water. I didn't realize that I had left the nipples in the water too long until I tried feeding Lindsay and realized that they had all sealed shut. Panic! Michael went out to get new nipples at the pharmacy, but we didn't know how to stop it from happening again. After much trial and error, we discovered that if you boil the nipples with round toothpicks in the holes, you solve the problem.

It is considered bad luck in the Jewish religion to set up a baby's room before the baby is born. While I am usually superstitious, there was no way I was heading into these uncharted waters unprepared. The room was fully set up with custom-designed bedding that matched the colourful wood-cut whimsical animals that hung on the wall. I had diapers, wipes, ointments, and a slew of onesies and sleepers.

I was ready for anything, but I quickly learned that my Type A personality was not a good fit with newborn parenting.

How can I keep on top of everything at work while also taking care of this tiny thing that was completely reliant on me to survive? It was a lot to manage. The day I got home from the hospital, I had to approve images from a photo shoot for a fashion client. In those days, you literally had to review hundreds of images on long strips of film with a magnifying loop. I could barely see straight but there was a deadline, so I climbed into bed and did what I had to do in between feedings, crying (Lindsay, not me), and diaper changes.

And then there was that new client pitch, four days postpartum. I put on one of the A-line mini dresses but the only tights I could find were maternity. I hastily put them on and headed to the meeting. When I got out of the car, the crotch of the tights had dropped below the hemline of my dress. In the parking lot, I hiked up my dress and pulled up the tights. They were so long that I had to pull them over my boobs. I did the meeting. I never heard from them. Fuckers.

I assumed that my mother would take care of meals and the laundry, but that did not seem to fall under her purview. I would wake up from a much-needed nap and ask her what was for dinner. She would tell me that she hadn't arranged anything and leave me to take care of it.

My parents did buy gourmet frozen lasagnas from a high-end grocer near our house, but there was only so much lasagna we could eat. My father and grandmother weren't sure what to do with themselves. My mother was essentially in charge, but really, the only thing she cared about was holding Lindsay.

I just couldn't seem to get on top of the situation. I was passing huge blood clots; my boobs were like two excruciatingly painful rocks for days after my milk came in because I wasn't breastfeeding. The laundry was piling up. At 4 p.m., I was still in pyjamas and the bottles weren't sterilized. I was trying to create this idyllic situation for my mother and grandmother. I wanted to look like I had it all together. For THEM. Epic failure.

My in-laws arrived in town a few days later. They were staying at a hotel that I booked for them that turned out to be horrible. My mother-in-law and I had gone through some rocky patches in our relationship, but these were desperate times, so I made a decision. I asked my mother-in-law to come stay at the house. My in-laws already had several grandchildren, so they knew the drill.

My mother-in-law was keen to jump in, and I clearly needed the help.

We had run out of beds, so my mother-in-law slept with me in our queen size bed and Michael moved to a sofa in the living room. My father-in-law remained at the horrible hotel. My mother-in-law was a lifesaver, and I think my mother was secretly relieved as well.

Interestingly, my mother wasn't freaked out by Lindsay crying. She actually calmed me down during those hours-long screaming sessions. But after a few days, it became obvious to me that it was going to be easier to figure everything out without my mother's "help." I had a discussion with my father and suggested that maybe it was time for them to leave. He enthusiastically agreed. Two years later, when Alex was born, my parents did not stay with us and very generously paid for a round-the-clock nurse to help take care of him for two weeks. Live and learn.

I began therapy for the first time when Lindsay was six weeks old. I resented my mother for putting me in a version of new motherhood that she herself had experienced. She did not have a "normal childhood" to emulate. In a very different way, neither did I.

There was a spectrum of issues to slog through. There were the "quirky" minor anxieties that I inherited and didn't want to pass on—fear of highway driving, unplugging electric appliances that might catch fire, repeatedly checking that I locked the front door when I left home, not letting my children get frozen at the dentist when they had cavities to fill. And then there were the "doozies"—physical safety, separation anxiety, criticism, anger, the overwhelming need to control a universe that could not be controlled.

The biggest difference in our approach to mothering was that I understood these were my issues to deal with, not my child's. My mother did not have that insight. There was no way, no matter how much pretzel-bending I would have done, that I could have delivered the reassurances that she needed to overcome her fears.

I knew I had to learn to subvert my desire to turn Lindsay into my version of who I wanted her to be. I needed, instead, to learn how to let her grow into who she wanted to be.

I found it baffling that so many first-time moms seemed to be weathering the storm better than I was. Was I somehow deficient? And while I will acknowledge that there are some women, like my cousin Charlotte, who love the newborn stage, I was not one of them. As women, I think we do a great disservice to other mothers when we sugar-coat how we feel and put rose-coloured glasses on our experiences. I would have felt less like I was failing if I had known it wasn't easy for other moms either.

Having a newborn is fucking impossible. I was brutally honest about how I was struggling and, more often than not, my admission gave other mothers permission to admit that they were having a hard time, too. Why do we feel this pressure to make it seem like we are perfect? It's okay to say we are not okay. It's okay to ask for help. I didn't know how I was going to survive the exhaustion. And I was one of the lucky ones. I had a healthy baby and money to get whatever we needed.

Entrepreneurs don't have the luxury of taking a maternity leave. I had to get back to work as soon as possible but I hadn't even started looking for a nanny. I don't know what I was waiting for, it was so unlike me to be unprepared. So, I sounded the alarm, like the dogs barking in *101 Dalmations*, and Nelsie came into our lives. She was referred by a friend of a friend and started working with us when Lindsay was three weeks old. I remember leaving Lindsay alone with her for the first time just to go to the pharmacy. It was so strange walking out of the house without Lindsay, a diaper bag, and a stroller.

Thanks to Nelsie, I was able to go back to work full-time (well, more than full-time) when Lindsay was five weeks old. Nelsie arrived at 8 a.m. and left at 6 p.m. Lindsay was usually asleep when I got home, but she would wake up at 6:05 p.m. and shriek until midnight. Colic. I was a walking zombie at work. Deborah told me years later that I was completely impossible to deal with in those first few months and that if we hadn't had a personal relationship, she would have been out the door. She certainly would have been justified.

I had bitten off way more than I could chew. There was a complex mix of things driving me that I didn't understand at the time. Part of it was arrogance. I believed I could keep all the balls in the air. I needed to keep all the balls in the air because my self-esteem was so closely tied to looking like I could do it all. And I wanted to make my father proud, because it did not feel like my mother ever would be.

Just after Lindsay was born, I was asked to join the board of Fashion Cares, a massive dinner and fashion show that raised money for the AIDS Committee of Toronto. The entire fashion community, retailers, designers, and beauty brands all banded together. The HIV/AIDS epidemic was raging. If you worked in the fashion industry, you bore witness to the ravages of AIDS up close. It was a terrifying time.

My favourite makeup artist was Pierre Tetrault, and I hired him for all my photo shoots. He was incredibly talented and hilarious. One day, he showed up on set and I knew. He didn't have to say anything. He had the look. In those days, AIDS was a death sentence. A few months later, he was dead. I couldn't say no to Fashion Cares, no matter what was going on in my life.

It was an overwhelming commitment. There were weekly evening meetings. In the three weeks leading up to the event, Deborah and I were putting in fourteen-hour days. I basically only saw Lindsay in the morning. She was asleep by the time I got home.

A few days before the event, one of the major sponsors let us know that they would be bringing in Claudia Schiffer as a guest of honour. Claudia was at the top of the heap of supermodels. It was my job to greet her when she arrived and run the press conference. Because it was so last minute, it was a mad scramble to put everything in place, which meant even longer hours away from home. This was the life I had chosen, without any thought as to how it would affect me or my family. I struggled behind the scenes, and then, "It's showtime folks."

On the evening of the event, I stepped outside at the appointed time to meet Claudia's car. It was May, but it was freezing that night. I was wearing a black crepe slip dress with thigh-high slits all around the bottom. Claudia arrived thirty minutes late because she couldn't decide what to wear. Any excitement I had about meeting her was replaced by hypothermia.

And then Claudia stepped out of the car. It was like she was surrounded by an aura of sunshine. She was stunning. I walked ahead of her, leading her to the press conference. Flashbulbs were going off like it was the Fourth of July. All I could think about was the media wondering who the troll (me) was walking ahead of this goddess (Claudia).

I continued my breakneck-speed life. When Lindsay was sixteen months old, I finally regained some semblance of control. It was short-lived. I know . . . here's an idea . . . why don't I get pregnant again!?!

The journey was even harder the second time. OverCat was in full swing. The 24/7 nausea returned. I had a one-and-a-half-year-old. I just kept adding balls.

I don't even remember the first two years after Alex was born. It's all just a blur. Nelsie was supposed to leave at six o'clock each day, but I was constantly calling to tell her I was running late. She was always understanding. I kept powering through. I was also doing a fair bit of travelling for work, which meant more time away from the kids. There was no time to think about whether or not I was being a good mother. I was barely able to keep my head above water.

When I was with my kids, I was thinking about work. When I was at work, I was missing my kids and feeling guilt. This was the world I had chosen, a restless existence where I always felt like I was coming up short.

I had fallen into the supermom trap. Two babies in two years while running a business. I was regaled by admiring choruses of "I don't know how you do it!" I know how I did it, I nearly lost my mind. That's how I fucking did it. I would literally cry Friday afternoons before I left the office in anticipation of forty-eight uninterrupted hours of childcare duties. Does that make me a bad mother? If I was able to do it all again, would I follow the same path? Absolutely not. I think—at least I hope—that my kids didn't suffer in the equation. I certainly did.

Years later when I discussed this period of my life with my therapist, she shared an interesting observation—I chose to live my life in diametric opposition of my mother. WHOA. Everything clicked into place. Of course that's what I was doing. I was critical of how she lived her sedentary life, so I subconsciously chose to do the exact opposite. But I was trapped. There was no way for me to step off the speedway.

There are always defining moments in a business. One happened on a random Friday afternoon. I picked up the ringing phone. The voice on the other end of the line said, "Hi, it's Joe Mimran from Club Monaco." I nearly fell off my chair. Joe Mimran was important. He was a retail legend. How did he even know who I was? Could I come in for a meeting? Hell yes.

Here's a tip. When you are meeting with a designer or a retail brand, you should always wear their clothes, or shoes, or accessories to that meeting. Yes, it can get expensive, but it makes a strong first impression. For the Mimran meeting, I bought a light brown nubby wool shift dress, which I paired with a black wool turtleneck, black opaque tights (not maternity), and black high-heeled booties.

Joe was lovely. Club Monaco had recently leased a historic, three-storey building on Bloor Street, Toronto's designer shopping mecca. They wanted to throw a pre-construction party in the space. Retailers do that to create buzz for a project. He told me there were three agencies participating in the pitch. OverCat, another larger, well-established agency in Toronto, and a publicist from New York. I didn't land the account. They went with the publicist from New York.

As a business owner, you have to learn to accept the losses graciously. Three weeks before the party, I received another call from Joe. The New York publicist was a disaster! Could I please come in as back up? They weren't going to fire the publicist because the optics would be bad, but they needed someone to actually do the work.

The New York publicist looked like he was hosting the party, but we organized everything. The fully stocked bars manned by attractive bartenders, beautiful passed hors d'oeuvres, personalized tours of what the space would look like after it was renovated. Following the event, OverCat kept the account and opened Club Monaco's first flagship store in New York. Joe's legacy continued to grow. Eventually, Club Monaco was acquired by Ralph Lauren. Joe continues to build successful retail ventures.

Meanwhile, back at the ranch, I had enrolled my kids in a ton of activities. Because I could not find a full-day nursery program, I sent them to two different schools, one in the morning and one in the afternoon, which meant double the drop-off and pick-ups. Nelsie was very, very busy.

Michael started travelling internationally for business—Dubai, Pakistan, Sri Lanka, Egypt. He travelled every six weeks and would be gone for two weeks each time. At first, I found it impossible, but eventually I got used to doing it all in the evenings and on weekends.

By the time the kids were ten and eight, Lindsay was studying ballet at the National Ballet School and Alex was playing Triple A hockey. This meant five nights a week of commitments for each of them. Michael was constantly leaving work early to ferry Alex to hockey. Nelsie would bring Lindsay to me at the office where I would feed her, take her to dance, go back to the office, and then back to dance to pick her up. I didn't get home until after 9 p.m. I was working twelve-hour days.

My mother was visiting Toronto when she made an interesting observation about my life. We were sitting in the kitchen of a new house Michael and I purchased that overlooked a huge indoor swimming pool. She was having her morning tea, and we were enjoying a rare, peaceful moment. "It seems to me that if nothing goes wrong, your life is almost manageable," she said. "But if something does, it spins out of control." She was absolutely right. And it always felt like one thing or another was spinning out of control. Midnight runs to the hospital when Alex had croup. Lindsay getting mono the weekend of Alex's Bar Mitzvah. Alex falling down the stairs, breaking his arm, and needing surgery. Lindsay getting head lice and giving it to me and Alex. Our house being robbed.

And of course, I wasn't exactly cutting myself any slack. As a professional event planner, I felt that there was an expectation that my kids' birthday parties would be extravaganzas. There was Alex's second birthday party in a children's event space where my brother dressed up as Batman (who Alex was obsessed with). Lindsay's sixth birthday party, where a reptile company came in and the kids played with snakes and lizards. Lindsay and Alex's joint birthday party when they were eight and six, featuring a Barbie impersonator who gave the girls manicures while the boys staged play fights with a Power Ranger impersonator.

For Lindsay's tenth birthday, I decided to go all out. In my world, that meant having a domesticated tiger come to the house. It seemed like a really cool idea until a limo pulled into the driveway and a giant tiger emerged. The kids were allowed to pet the tiger and get a picture with him. In retrospect, it was a very stupid, life-endangering event. But go big or go home.

We also gave Lindsay an adorable chocolate lab puppy that the kids named Tia Maria (because why not add a dog in to the mix). My mother was terrified of dogs, likely due to the German Shepherds that roamed Auschwitz. As a result, I had never had a dog before, and we were ill-prepared for the chaos that Tia wrought. We got her around the same time as the release of the book *Marley and Me.* Tia made Marley look like the best-behaved dog in the world.

One night, shortly after we moved into a new house, Alex and I went out to buy a toaster oven. Michael was in Dubai and Lindsay was at sleep-away camp. When we came home, I heard the sound of rushing water. We were having some work done and a door that should have been closed was left open, giving Tia access to a water valve which she apparently chewed on enough to flood the basement.

I called Michael and told him that was it. Tia had to go. Eight-year-old Alex was sitting next to me and begged me to keep Tia. Which, of course, we did.

Tia was obsessed with licking the dirty plates in the dishwasher, which seemed harmless enough until her collar got stuck on one of the plastic spikes. She got totally spooked and pulled out the entire rack full of dishes. Lindsay and I were both in the kitchen and heard the noise but initially couldn't understand what was going on until we saw Tia, attached to the dish rack, tearing around the room with dishes flying everywhere and breaking. Lindsay finally corralled her, but not before she gashed her knee on a broken dish.

Both my parents were understandably wary of Tia. On one visit, my mother was seated at the kitchen table when Nelsie came back from a dog walk. Tia immediately bolted over to my mother and started jumping all over her. My mother was remarkably calm. "Mom, how come you aren't panicking?" I asked. She replied, "I close my eyes and hope for the best."

I was struck by her answer. There is an expression, "Hope is not a strategy," but during the war, when everything was out of her and my grandmother's control, hope was the only strategy. In the safe haven of her life in Canada, shouldn't she have been able to rely on her resources more than just the spectre of hope? Didn't she have an obligation to do better? To be better? Or was shutting out the darkness the best she could do?

The agency just kept getting busier and busier. Events in New York for Sarah Jessica Parker, Jennifer Lopez, and Jon Bon Jovi. Yes, he is even better looking in person and totally charming. Celine Dion in Vegas. A press trip to Sweden for IKEA.

Even in this glamourous world that I found myself wading in, death was still nipping at my Chanel two-tone boots. I was doing a lot of pro bono work and was approached by the executive director of a charitable organization that was working with a sexual abuse whistleblower named Martin Kruze.

Kruze was a promising young hockey player. From the time he was thirteen, he was sexually abused by two staff members associated with Toronto's then hockey mecca, Maple Leaf Gardens. This occurred between 1975 and 1982.

Of course, I already knew his name from the plethora of articles that had come out about him. I was asked to help develop a communications strategy around the work Martin was doing to raise awareness about child sexual abuse. I only met Martin once. We had a meeting in my office over a brunch of bagels, lox, and cream cheese.

He was such a sweet man. And so brave. And he had a great appetite. He had never had lox before. In private discussions with the executive director, I expressed how strongly I felt about him and the work they were doing. She told me that going public and heading into a trial is a very dangerous time psychologically for abuse victims. Martin was so dedicated to helping others, I was sure she was wrong.

In 1997, one of the abusers plead guilty to sexual assault charges related to twenty-four boys. He was only sentenced to two years less a day. Three days later, Martin walked onto the Bloor Street Viaduct in the heart of Toronto at 11 a.m. and jumped. I didn't know at the time that he had already made several suicide attempts, including six days before, when doctors found him on the ledge of a Toronto hospital where he was being treated. I didn't know he had been going through ten years of intensive therapy.

The night before the funeral, I received a call from the executive director asking for my help. A number of people speaking at the funeral were sexual assault survivors who had not gone public. There were also people who were in hiding from their abusers who would be in attendance. Because the funeral would obviously be a media circus, it was crucial that the names and images of these speakers were not made public. I was asked to manage the media and explain that no names or images from the funeral could appear in the press, which I did, and to their credit, they respected.

It was an open casket funeral. I had never been to an open casket funeral. Jewish funerals are always closed casket. I remember being struck that Martin somehow didn't look real. More like a replica made by Madame Tussaud.

Eventually, more than eighty men and women came forward with their stories of abuse related to The Maple Leaf Gardens case.

There are people you meet, however fleetingly, that never leave you.

And then there is Karen, who came into my life unexpectedly in the late 1990s and has stayed there ever since. Karen's best friend was a junior at the agency. We needed some last-minute help packing up boxes for a big media mailer, and the junior suggested

Karen. She had recently graduated from university and was helping look after her grandfather who was very ill.

In the two days that Karen was there, I was immediately impressed by her. She was so calm and such a hard worker. Her friend, the junior, was not really working out, so I decided to hire Karen full-time and let her best friend go. The friend was unimpressed.

Karen eventually became my second-in-command. I loved her. We became a huge part of each other's lives. When her boyfriend John wanted to propose, he called me and asked if there was a way I could find out Karen's ring size for the engagement ring. I do love a secret mission.

Part of our job at the agency was to pull merchandise from clients to be featured in newspaper and magazine fashion shoots. Aha! In addition to the clothing, I picked out rings in different sizes and walked into Karen's office with them. I asked if she could try them on so I could see what they would look like on a model's hand. Success! I jotted down her size and let John know.

One day, about eighteen months after she got married, she complained that her right wrist was stiff. She and John had been painting their new townhouse, and she assumed it was from that. But it just kept getting worse and she was having trouble using it. Then she started to limp, on the same side. By the time she finally decided to see a doctor, she couldn't type or write with her right hand.

The doctors were puzzled as to what it was but told her that she needed to be admitted to the hospital the following week. If her symptoms worsened, she was advised to go to a hospital emergency room immediately.

We had a huge Bat Mitzvah party that we had been hired to do that weekend. Karen was in charge because I was going to be at Naomi's daughter's Bat Mitzvah, which fell on the same night. I didn't say anything to our staff about Karen, although I knew that come Monday, Karen would have to go on temporary sick leave.

She was subjected to a battery of tests. John stayed at the hospital all day, so I would visit at lunchtime to give him a break. I told the staff that Karen was dealing with a personal issue and lied about where I was going. Five days after she was admitted, she told me that they had done yet another blood test, but she wasn't sure what this one was for. I told her I would ask my dad and call her when I got back to the office. At that point, she thought the diagnosis was leaning toward MS. Okay. Not the worst possible diagnosis, but obviously life-changing.

After I spoke with my dad, I called her room to let her know what he told me. When she answered the phone, she was sobbing so hard that I couldn't understand her. She had just been told she had an inoperable brain tumour. She picked up the phone because she thought it was her mother calling.

The doctors weren't sure whether the tumour was malignant or benign. But with a brain tumour, that distinction hardly matters—its growth alone can cause catastrophic damage. I asked every doctor I knew what they thought her prognosis was, and they all said the same thing. Even if brain tumours go into remission, at some point, they will likely start to grow again. I refused to believe this was the case. She would be one of the lucky ones who would be fine. Karen was twenty-nine at the time.

She underwent a series of treatments including radiation. And it worked! She regained her mobility. She chose not to come back to work but we remained close. When my parents died, she felt like she didn't do enough to be there for me. There was nothing more she could have done. I always knew that she was there for me.

Karen and John were given the all-clear to start a family, but she couldn't get pregnant. After trying for a few years, they discovered that Karen had a chemical imbalance that was an easy fix, and she became pregnant almost immediately. The week she found out she was pregnant, her doctors told her that the tumour had begun growing again.

The suggested treatment meant that she would have to terminate the pregnancy and would not ever be able to get pregnant again. Her team of oncologists told her that they would support her in whatever decision she made. Karen and John decided they wanted to have the baby. As the pregnancy progressed, all her originals symptoms returned. I remember having lunch with her near the end of the pregnancy, watching her with her big belly, limping along the street.

Karen gave birth to Charlie, her son, via a planned C-section. She was to start treatment again soon after. I'm not sure if anyone knows exactly what went wrong, but possibly the tumour ruptured and leaked into her spinal column. Karen became totally paralyzed on her right side. She was never able to feed or hold Charlie.

When Karen came home from the hospital, John set up a bed for her on the main floor of their townhouse. John, with some help from family and friends, looked after a newborn while his thirty-five-year-old wife was dying in the family room. Then John called to tell me that the doctors had told them there was nothing further that could be done.

I began visiting Karen once a week with an ex OverCat employee who was also close with Karen. Karen was such a fighter. Her doctors told her that she likely wouldn't make it to Christmas, which was a few months away. Visiting her was heartbreaking but I am so grateful that we got to spend that time together. She told me that she didn't want to live, that she felt that she was such a burden to everyone.

The new year came and Karen was still with us, but she was deteriorating. For some reason, Karen decided that she wanted her wedding dress dry-cleaned before she passed away. John entrusted me with that task.

She told me she was considering an open casket funeral, but only if she still looked "sassy." In early March, they decided to move Karen to hospice care. John asked if I wanted to see her. She wasn't conscious on that last visit. I spoke to her; I told that I loved her. Karen died on March 11. She was thirty-six. Her son Charlie was eleven months old.

John called me a few days before the funeral and asked me if I would order the wreath that was to be placed on the casket. He told me Karen wanted to make sure it wasn't tacky and knew that I would order something beautiful. I chose an all-white floral wreath. The casket was open. She still looked sassy.

There are very few people in this world that I admire as much as John. He never wavered in his care and love for Karen. I was determined to stay a part of John and Charlie's lives. John asked me if I would come with him for Charlie's first pictures with Santa. We met at a mall close to their home. I asked John if I could buy Charlie a chocolate chip cookie to eat while we were in line waiting to see Santa.

John and I were so engrossed in our conversation that we didn't realize that the chocolate from the giant cookie had melted all over Charlie. He was covered in chocolate! John had forgotten to bring wipes, so I had to ask the mothers around us if they had any extra.

They looked at John and I like we should not be entrusted with a child. We managed to get Charlie mostly cleaned up, but the second John put him on Santa's lap, Charlie started to shriek. And kept shrieking, which the photo captured perfectly.

Two years ago, John married Angela, one of Karen's best friends who had been divorced many years earlier. Angela has a son a few years older than Charlie. They consider themselves brothers.

At the wedding, John sat Michael and I with Karen's family. I didn't know most of them. They wanted to hear about Karen back then, before she was sick. I made them laugh with my stories of our adventures, but I cried the whole time.

Karen never got to fully spread her wings, but she left a tremendous legacy of love. I think of her all the time, but especially on March 11, when we lost an angel.

I'm Not Ready to Let You Go

MY GRANDMOTHER OUTLIVED HER PARENTS, her siblings, and three husbands. She was a breathtaking example of the strength of the human spirit.

After Jack died, my grandmother began renting out the second bedroom of her apartment. It was a reasonable solution to help with the loneliness. The most infamous roommate was Annette. Annette had undergone a lobotomy. One day, my grandmother called my father because Annette was talking to the radiator. That was the end of the roommates.

From the time I was born, my grandmother was a permanent fixture in my life. She would come over every day to help my mother. She was our babysitter when my parents went out on Saturday nights, and she was left in charge when they went out of town.

Before we moved into the house in Westmount, we lived in a duplex across the street from a sprawling park. She often took me there and pushed me on the baby swings. There was also a wading pond. One day, for reasons I can't recall, I was all dressed up and my grandmother took me to watch the kids splashing in the shallow water. Somehow, I tripped down the two little steps and toppled into the pool. I was in no physical danger, but my outfit was ruined. I thought she would be angry, but instead she laughed as she rushed her sopping wet charge back home.

I was happy to spend as much time as I could with my grandmother, begging my parents to let me stay over at her apartment on weekends and sleep in the extra bedroom that once belonged to her roommates.

My grandmother never seemed bitter or tormented by her past. Even as a young child, I could see the profound differences between my mother and my grandmother.

Despite the unimaginable losses that my grandmother experienced, she didn't seem to haul her trauma around the way my mother did. She was a generally happy, optimistic person who seemed more at peace in the world than my mother. She was steadfast, dependable, and a source of unconditional love.

My grandmother's best friends in Montreal were Yetka and Itzka Biderman, a couple who lived around the corner from her. They were warm, wonderful people who also survived the Holocaust. I asked my mother why the Bidermans never had children. Apparently, Yetka had become pregnant at some point during the war and had an abortion. She could not conceive after that.

Yetka was very short and walked with a pronounced limp. I don't know if the cause of her limp happened before or during the war. She had waist-length hair that she rolled into coils, which sat atop her head like grey-streaked cinnamon buns.

Itzka was startlingly handsome with a shock of grey hair and luminescent blue eyes. My brother and I loved them like grandparents, and they treated us like their grandchildren. They were included in all our family gatherings. It was Yetka who had smuggled the diamond in my future engagement ring out of Europe in her tooth.

In the 1970s, when the politics in Quebec became increasingly fraught, the Bidermans decided to move to Toronto. They had lived in Montreal for thirty years, but they were frightened of what was happening in Quebec. Despite the move, my grandmother and the Bidermans remained the best of friends.

One night, many years after they had moved, Itzka called and I answered the phone. He told me Yetka had had a massive coronary and died. It was up to my father to tell my grandmother. We all knew this would devastate her. I clearly remember standing next to my father in the kitchen when he called my grandmother to tell her, "*Yetka iz geshtorben.*" Yetka is dead, in Yiddish. I heard my grandmother screaming in grief through the phone.

My grandmother immediately flew to Toronto. This was around the same time that I'd started dating Michael and was frequently visiting Toronto. While I wasn't in town on the day of the funeral, I was there for the Shiva. Jews sit Shiva (the Hebrew word for the number seven) for seven days after someone dies. It begins right after the burial. Friends and family visit the Shiva mourners to pay their respect and to serve as a distraction for the mourners' grief.

I didn't go. It was more important to me to spend time with Michael. My grandmother knew I was in Toronto, but I never called or visited the Shiva. When she asked me why I didn't go, I had no good reason. She let me know she was very disappointed in me. I think it may be the only time in my life that I disappointed my grandmother. I am still ashamed of my behaviour.

My grandmother spent a lot of time in Toronto after Yetka died and she stayed in the apartment with Itzka. I think my grandmother felt an obligation to look after Itzka, but she also cared deeply for him, as he did for her. A few months later, my grandmother announced that they had gotten married. By this point, she had been a widow for many decades. I think they truly loved each other. They both seemed very happy. Once again, these survivors rebuilt their lives.

By this time, I had moved to Toronto. It became a ritual for me to have weekly Sunday lunches at their apartment. Michael would occasionally join as well. He loved my grandmother. I didn't have a car at the time, and it took an hour by bus each way. My grandmother would prepare a giant feast of soup, chicken, potatoes, cauliflower, and cookies. I brought the leftovers home. Inevitably, after lunch, my stomach would be upset by all the heavy food. The bus ride home was usually followed by a mad dash to the bathroom.

My mother was aware that I did these weekly trips and thought I was a hero for undertaking these time-consuming visits. She looked at it as an obligation. I had a different point of view. I did not know how much time I had left with my grandmother, and I didn't want to look back and regret that I didn't do everything I could to show her how much I loved her. I felt that demonstrating my love and commitment to her while she was alive was much more important than heaping accolades on her after she passed away. I also never wanted to disappoint her again.

Itzka was becoming very frail so it was decided that it would make more sense for them to return to Montreal. I helped my grandmother pack up their Toronto apartment. We went through old family pictures, my grandmother pointing out long dead family members, both of us crying.

My grandmother was a bit more forthcoming about the Holocaust than my mother, but she still didn't talk about it a lot. She did share two stories with me about Auschwitz. The first took place before my mother was moved to the Kinderlager and involved a rumour she had heard that the Nazis were coming to collect all the children and exterminate them. She took my mother and hid in an outhouse for three days. When they emerged, my mother was one of very few children left. The second was the story about begging for food at the kitchen fence.

At one point, we started talking about my mother, who was still making me miserable about my move to Toronto. My grandmother startled me when she said, "Your mother is not a well woman." I was shocked.

I had known for a long time that my mother was "off," but somehow, when my grandmother said it out loud, it became something bigger. I realized that other people saw it, too. My grandmother was acknowledging that my mother had mental health challenges.

Now that my grandmother and Itzka were back in Montreal, my parents had to take on more responsibility. Doctors' appointments, grocery shopping, and spending time with them. My father, as always, was a devoted son-in-law, but he was also a very busy doctor. My mother begrudgingly did what she had to do. Itzka became ill a few years after they moved back and had to be hospitalized. My grandmother began spending her days at the hospital, which was just up the hill from their apartment.

Itzka was on a floor with other geriatric patients, mostly men. The wives formed a unique bond, and in a strange way, my grandmother flourished in this new arrangement. It gave her something to do every day.

It was winter, and even though it was a short walk to the hospital, my mother tried to discourage my grandmother from going. She was terrified that my grandmother would slip on the ice and break something. Not because she was worried about my grandmother, but because she was worried that she would have to take care of her. My mother never came out and said that, but I knew that's what she was thinking. She would rather that my grandmother stay home and Itzka be alone in the hospital. She never offered to help my grandmother get to the hospital or pick her up.

Itzka remained in the hospital for a few months and never recovered. When he died, I flew home to be with my grandmother. My mother was doing a pretty good job of ignoring her. I spent the day before the funeral at my grandmother's apartment. My mother never came over. Jewish funerals are closed casket, but family members can request a private visit with an open casket before the service. My grandmother wanted to see Itzka one last time. My parents were vehemently against it, so I told my grandmother I would do it with her.

The funeral home was walking distance from her apartment. I told her I would go into the room with her to see Itzka, but right before we went in, she told me not to come in with her. She was protecting me.

Now, my grandmother was living alone again in her Montreal apartment. Most of her friends had already died, and the ones who were still alive weren't that mobile. She was still sharp as a tack, but her body was starting to fail her. It was becoming increasingly difficult for her to go out on her own, which meant she was stuck at home by herself a great deal of the time.

My mother wasn't really interested in becoming a caregiver to her elderly mother. My grandmother was certainly aware of it; she mentioned it frequently on our phone calls, telling me that my mother didn't visit her very often and when she did visit, my grandmother sensed that she couldn't wait to leave. I was furious with my mother. How could she abandon her mother like this? When I spoke with my mother about it or, more accurately, chastised her about it, she reassured me that she was doing a great job and that my grandmother's complaints were unwarranted.

One year, there was a terrible ice storm in Montreal and everyone lost power for three days. Of course, I was worried about my parents and my grandmother. They were all being stubborn and refusing to leave their homes, choosing instead to bundle up and wait it out. I was actively trying to convince all of them to go somewhere that had electricity. I wanted them to take a train to Toronto, but nobody would budge. They said they were all doing fine. This seemed extremely unlikely, and I was panicked that they would freeze to death. Years later, they would joke about it.

I will give my parents the benefit of the doubt that they tried to convince my grandmother to come stay with them and she refused. Personally, I would have dragged her out of her apartment if I was there. I would not have been able to let her stay alone in the dark and cold.

I was concerned about the way this whole situation was evolving. I started having discussions with my grandmother about moving into an assisted living facility. She was a very social person, and I thought she would fare much better with people around. I begged her to consider it. She would still have her own apartment unit, but she wouldn't have to prepare meals, and she would have company. Most importantly, I wanted her to make her own decision and not be in a situation where we were forced to decide for her. I wanted her to be in control of her own destiny.

After many months of badgering, my grandmother acquiesced and agreed to look at some options. I didn't want my parents to know what I was doing so I arranged to go to Montreal when they were out of town. I booked two appointments for us to see potential residences. I didn't like the first one but thought the second was a good option. She decided pretty quickly that she would stay where she was. She wasn't receptive to making a change. She had a litany of complaints as to why those places were no good. Maybe I was trying to mitigate my guilt about not being in Montreal to help take care of her.

I wanted her to move back to Toronto. There was an apartment building very close to my house, but she wouldn't entertain it.

A few months later, at my parents' house, my mother confronted me. "Bubby told me you took her to see some assisted living facilities." Oh shit. I froze. I thought my mother would be furious with me. "If you could convince her to move, it would be the happiest day of my life." I was stunned. It was clear to me that this was about my mother's happiness and not what was best for my grandmother. I was so disappointed in my mother. That she could vocalize that sentiment and not see how self-involved it was shocked me. It also underscored the complexity of the mother/daughter/granddaughter/grandmother relationships between my grandmother, my mother, Lindsay, and me. My grandmother could be sharply and vocally critical of my mother, who was woefully ill equipped to deal with it. For the women in my family, criticism was like a hot potato that we passed down from one generation to the next.

My grandmother was very frugal and did not like to spend money. Because my grandmother didn't drive, my mother often did her grocery shopping. One time, my mother bought some kosher chicken for my grandmother only to be lectured that she should have bought it somewhere else where it was less expensive. Exasperated, my mother said, "You know, before I die, I'd like you to tell me that I did something right."

She disapproved of my mother spending so much money on clothes. She found it frivolous that my parents spent money on family vacations, though I suspect part of it may have had to do with the fear of something happening to us. It became a family tradition to fudge the truth and tell Bubby something cost half the actual price.

Despite the fact that my mother buckled under her mother's negative comments, my mother could not curb her criticism of me.

No matter what I achieved, I never felt like my mother was proud of me. Eunice, who was extremely close with my mother, told me that she would point out how creative and accomplished I was whenever my mother would talk negatively about me, but my mother didn't bite.

I often thought that when I was out of my mother's line of vision, she relegated me to suspended animation. She never really understood the magnitude of my life because the parts that didn't involve her weren't relevant. She knew, of course, that I worked really hard and was a dedicated mother. But she didn't understand how difficult that was, and it never stopped her from criticizing me for my choices.

I, in turn, was critical of Lindsay. There are times I should have kept my mouth shut. I wanted her to get better grades. I wanted her to be more dedicated to her dance training. I lectured her when she gained weight. I know . . . horrible.

What is our obligation to try to clean up our own messes and stop them from spilling over onto the people we love? How much should we carry ourselves and what is too much to unload on others?

On the other hand, I had an incredible relationship with my grandmother, as Lindsay did with hers. In sixteen years, not once did my mother heap any of her bullshit on her granddaughter. She was able to bury her trauma deep enough to allow them to have a beautiful relationship. Lindsay cherished her relationship with her grandmother.

My grandmother was still steadfastly refusing to entertain any alternatives to her current living situation. I know it's not uncommon for elderly people to resist moving into seniors' facilities. I'm sure it's terrifying to give up control and know that this is the last stop. If they won't move willingly, then it's just a waiting game for a crisis. And that is exactly what happened.

One day, she was standing on a chair in her kitchen trying to change a light bulb and she fell. The women living in the apartment below her heard a big crash and called the superintendent. They found my grandmother on the floor and called an ambulance. She had fractured her back. She was admitted to the hospital for a few weeks, followed by some time in a rehab facility. She eventually fully recovered, but she didn't want to go back to her apartment and asked to move into an assisted living facility. She was now too frightened to live on her own. I don't know if my parents ever discussed having my grandmother move into their house, but I suspect not.

She settled in quickly and was doing well there, as I knew she would. She had her own little apartment, and all her meals were served in a communal dining room. She was outgoing and made friends easily. She liked the food.

We spoke every Sunday morning at 9:30 a.m. During one of those calls, my grandmother told me that she had privately hired someone to give her a bath after our weekly calls. She said I was the only one who knew about it. She loved hot baths but could no longer navigate them herself.

Sunday, March 18, 2001. My grandmother and I spoke that morning. Then I went out for the day with my family. When I got home, there was a message from my dad to call home followed by several hang-ups. This was still in the era of answering machines. My father's voice sounded strange. I knew the hang-ups were because he was trying to reach me.

When I called him back, he told me that they had received a call from my grandmother's residence that she'd been scalded in the bathtub. It was serious and they had called an ambulance. My parents arrived at my grandmother's apartment just as they were taking her out on a stretcher. My mother said my grandmother smiled at her and then closed her eyes.

When we spoke, about eight hours after the incident, my grandmother had not regained consciousness. I don't know if I was in shock, or if my parents downplayed her condition, but for some reason, I decided not to fly to Montreal immediately. I would wait and see, praying that she would wake up and everything would be fine.

And there it was in action. The biggest gift my mother gave me—compartmentalization. The ability to appear normal and function seamlessly while your life is imploding. Don't let the world at large know that you aren't perfect. Nothing to see here folks. Move along.

My mother used to call me a sociopath because I was not destroyed by her relentless tirades. Her behaviour actually made me stronger and fearless, compelling me to lock away the portions I could not handle.

The next day, I went to work. My grandmother hadn't improved so I flew to Montreal that night. My parents and I spent the next two days at her bedside. No change.

Thursday, March 22. My mother woke me up early. The hospital had called. My grandmother wasn't doing well. We got into the car and headed to the hospital in the middle of a blizzard. My grandmother's organs were failing. That smile that she had given my mother as the paramedics loaded her into the ambulance had been her last conscious act. She never woke up again.

The three of us sat by her bedside and watched the numbers on the monitors drop. It was a completely surreal experience, watching this incredibly strong woman slowly slip away. I asked my parents to leave the room so I could say goodbye privately. I whispered in her ear that I was sorry. Sorry for everything that had happened to her. My parents each took their turns saying goodbye and then we watched the numbers drop to zero. My Bubby was gone.

While my parents were dealing with administrative issues, I checked my cell phone, which had been turned off. I had a message from the president of Hugo Boss, one of our clients. I called back from a lounge in the hospital and was briefed on an upcoming project. My grandmother, who I dearly loved, had been dead less than thirty minutes and I was taking a work call.

I was disgusted with myself. I felt like I was betraying her. I went straight into Energizer Bunny mode. Wind me up and send me out. It's what I was trained to do.

The blizzard raged on. I felt it was the universe mourning my grandmother. And then we did all the things you do when someone dies. Choose a casket, make funeral arrangements, write an obituary.

For some reason, I had not yet told my parents about my grandmother hiring someone to come in and give her Sunday morning baths. When I did tell them, they didn't believe me. They knew nothing about it. But I knew it was true.

So, what really happened? Did the caregiver not pay attention and put my grandmother in scalding hot water? Did my grandmother somehow turn on the hot water tap by herself? Was it a deliberate act by the caregiver? And why the fuck did a seniors' facility have water hot enough to kill someone?

I wanted to call the residence and tell them to keep the security footage from the camera in the hallway. I wanted to start an investigation. I wanted to know what happened.

My parents' reaction shocked me. They did not want to pursue it. In their opinion, it was an accident, and since she was eighty-six, she likely would have faced serious health concerns soon. They saw it as a relatively peaceful death. I was furious. My mother said it would be bad for my father as a doctor to be involved in the investigation of a healthcare facility. I knew that was a lie, my mother was just trying to say anything to get me to back down.

Because of the circumstances of her death, there was an autopsy, which delayed the funeral (in the Jewish religion, the funeral is supposed to happen within forty-eight hours). The funeral took place on March 25. The first Sunday in years that I had not spoken to my Bubby.

The coroner's report said my grandmother had boiled water on the stove for a bath and that was how she got scalded. I knew that wasn't what happened. It was clear that my parents were not going to pursue anything more. My grandmother was dead. They accepted it. There was a level of hysteria in my mother when I challenged her about it. I recognized this emotion. She employed it when she wanted me to drop something. What could I do? My mother had also lost someone she loved. I respected her wishes. I did nothing. I felt like I was betraying my grandmother.

March 18, the day of the accident. March 22, the day my grandmother died. March 25, the day of the funeral. Twenty-three years later, those dates still reverberate in my brain.

We were no longer a powerhouse of four generations of women who defeated all attempts to extinguish us. We were down a warrior. Our picture may be captured forever in the pages of *Kinderlager,* but in the real world, we were just three. I had never allowed myself to imagine a world without my grandmother. Or that seven years later, we would be reduced to two generations.

I thought my mother would fall apart when my grandmother died. But I was wrong, as I have been about so many other things regarding my mother. The Shiva was held at my parents' house. My mother's well-dressed friends arrived in droves. She played the perfect hostess.

I can understand how some people find this ritual comforting. I am not one of them. I resent this mourning protocol that turns death into a social activity. I didn't want to speak to anyone. I didn't want to see anyone. I just wanted my grandmother back. I left on the fourth day of the Shiva. I couldn't bear to be there another day. Dressing up and being polite when all I wanted to do was scream. I told my parents I needed to go home and be with my kids. They understood.

Several years earlier, my mother and my grandmother had filmed their stories for The Shoah Project. Steven Spielberg had undertaken this massive initiative to document the stories of as many Holocaust survivors as possible. I had never watched either of theirs.

On the day I came home from Montreal, I went into the upstairs den after I put the kids to bed, closed the door, and inserted the cassette into the VCR. My grandmother whirred to life in my parents' den where it was filmed.

The first question the interviewer asked my grandmother was: "Why do you think you survived?" Without missing a beat, she said: "Because God wanted me to." This was obviously something she had thought a lot about. I was surprised by her response. Although my grandmother had been born into a religious family in Poland, she was not particularly observant in Montreal. I wasn't aware of the depth of her spiritual beliefs.

In the weeks following her death, I resumed my normal activities, but when I was alone in my car, I would scream and cry.

With the small inheritance I received, I dedicated a classroom in my children's school to her. I was very lucky to have her in my life. She was miraculous. She survived Auschwitz and lived to see grandchildren and great grandchildren. She had a saying, "*Altz far di kinder*"—everything for the children. That was how she lived. That is her legacy.

I hope, somehow, she heard my final whispered words to her. I hope she knew how much I loved her; how much I still miss her, and how I still try to make her proud. I'm not sure that she would be happy about this book.

The Ripple Eclipse

"As paradoxical as it sounds, I am optimistic about the human race. Also, in the ability to rise from the ashes, attempt to rebuild shattered lives, and on some measure, succeed. Otherwise, why go on?

"What kind of person would I have been without the war? What would have been my strengths? What would have been my weaknesses? I like to think that I know where the scars are. Scars heal, but they are never as strong as the original fabric. It's been said that we're all in recovery. We've all been dropped on our heads. We're all the walking wounded on some level.

"I've always tried to use the war, as an experience which was really traumatic, to build, to learn, to heal. To become a better person. To have good balance, to put things in perspective, but I'm going to suffer. Whether it's my childhood or in my adult life, I'm going to take that suffering and learn something from it. It's not going to go to waste."

—From the transcript of the 1994 interviews with *Kinderlager* author Milton Nieuwsma. My mother was fifty-seven, fourteen years before her death.

My mother's volatility continued to dominate our family life. There was virtually nothing we could do to mitigate her fury. It would be up to her to wrestle with herself until she could finally regain some semblance of control. We waited like golfers on the green in a thunderstorm, hoping to avoid electrocution. That's just the way it was.

I always joke that "Hyams sight" is 20/20. There are things that happened that seemed innocuous at the time, but in retrospect, were huge red flags.

Three years before my mother died, her doctor found a node on her thyroid and recommended she have it removed. My father didn't want to inconvenience me and told me not to come in for the surgery, which I completely ignored. I was alone with her in the hospital room when she woke up from the surgery. I must have been reading because I didn't realize that she was awake until I heard her say, "I don't know why I've always been so hard on you." I sat there, stunned. Frozen on the uncomfortable metal chair. Her confession meant that, on some level, she knew how difficult she had made my life. I didn't acknowledge it, and we never spoke of it again. I don't know if she even remembered saying it.

I didn't know what do with her admission. I do believe that anaesthesia fucks with your mind. In my mother's case, it seemed to have opened some window of introspection, triggering her traumatic childhood memories, or perhaps amplifying feelings she was already experiencing. Something significant changed in my mother after that operation. The mania that she sometimes exhibited was now omnipresent. At first, I just assumed it would go away. But it only got worse in the years leading up to her death.

It showed up in various ways. One evening in the dead of winter, my parents planned to attend a lecture at their synagogue, which they did on a regular basis. Because the sidewalk was icy, my father dropped my mother off at the door and went to park the car. When he entered the synagogue, he was asked to join a minyan, which requires ten men to proceed with the prayers. That night, they only had nine.

When he did not show up to the lecture in a timely manner, my mother went into full-blown panic mode. My father told me she had run around the large synagogue like a lunatic trying to find him. She was terrified that something had happened to him. I don't know if she ever pictured what her life would look like if my father died, but I suspect that this profound fear got heaped on top of her mountain of existing anxieties.

She also started to renege on social engagements, which was very unusual for her. She bailed on Naomi's son Adam's Bar Mitzvah a few days before they were supposed to travel to Toronto. She said she wasn't feeling well.

Then, a few months later, my parents cancelled coming to Lindsay's Sweet Sixteen, two days before the party. Apparently, there was some sort of plumbing emergency at their house. It was a bizarre explanation that I did not believe.

She stopped seeing her friends, although she stayed connected with them by talking for hours on end over the phone. They didn't have call waiting and I was always getting a busy signal. She stopped grocery shopping and cooking.

There seemed to be an endless merry-go-round of physical ailments—back problems, foot issues, toothaches, tinnitus.

When I expressed my concern about my mother's behaviour to my father, the only thing he said to me was, "Holocaust survivors don't tend to age well." Cryptic and vague.

This was not new territory between my parents and me. They fudged the truth when they wanted to avoid dealing with a difficult subject head-on. These lies of omission did not have malicious intent; they were just an automatic default. They both lacked the acting skills required to pull off lying convincingly, insisting everything was okay when clearly it wasn't. Many, many times, their voices betrayed them over the phone. They refused to be forthcoming.

This created an air of mistrust and precluded us from having a true adult relationship. Maybe they thought they were protecting me, but I think it was more than that. They couldn't handle what was going on in their lives, and if they brought me into it, then they might have to actually deal with the issues. As long as it was just between them, they were free to make whatever misguided decisions they wanted to. No matter how many times I begged them to tell me the truth, they always deflected. I never knew what to believe. They actually tried to hide the fact that my paternal grandma Florence had died because there was an ice storm predicted in Montreal and they didn't want me to risk coming in for the funeral.

I learned later, from Eunice, that my father had been speaking to Max about how concerned he was regarding my mother's mental state.

The irony was that in both my personal and professional lives, I was someone that people turned to in a crisis. My friends knew I could be relied upon in extremely difficult situations, and I handled crisis communications strategy for huge corporate clients.

A year before they died, I was out for dinner in Montreal with my parents. While we were deciding what to order, my mother abruptly stood up, scooted over to the next table, hovered over the diners, and asked what they were eating. There was something frenetic about her behaviour. She was normally very polished in public.

I went back to Montreal a few weeks later and had lunch alone with my mother. I begged her to let me help her. Have groceries delivered, hire someone to cook and clean, do anything to make her feel less overwhelmed. She was like a broken record, shutting down every suggestion I made. She didn't want anyone in the house to help, and she wanted me to drop it. She was so insistent that I had no choice but to leave it alone for the time being.

The disturbing behaviour continued to escalate. One Saturday afternoon, I went to the office to catch up on work, as I often did. When I got there, I noticed my phone indicating that my mailbox was full, which was strange because I had just cleared it out the day before. I punched in the code, and the polite voice let me know that I had twenty-one unheard messages. I was sure I was the victim of some phone scam, but when I hit the play button to listen to my messages on speaker, my mother's voice filled the room.

I assume she thought I wouldn't hear the message until Monday. She was upset about something I did and didn't want to confront me directly. But she couldn't contain herself. Her solution was to leave me a message. She discovered that there was a three-minute time limit per message, so when she would get cut-off, she would simply call back and continue her diatribe. She even noted that she loved this newfound technological way to deliver her message with no interruption from me. In total, she rambled on for a full hour . . . in three-minute increments. I asked her to never do that again.

When I called her in August to make plans for Rosh Hashanah in late September, she told me she didn't want us to come in. We always stayed with my parents, but she told me that it was too much for her this year. We had NEVER missed spending Rosh Hashanah as a family. Something was seriously off. I was becoming increasingly alarmed about her decline, and worried about my father, who was dealing with it on his own.

I knew I had to find a way to overcome her objections and see for myself what was going on. It was too easy for her to brush off my concerns over the phone. After several arguments, she finally relented after I promised that we would stay in a hotel and I would arrange to have the Rosh Hashanah dinner delivered so that she wouldn't have to prepare anything.

Our first night in Montreal, we ate our catered dinner in my mother's designer blue, white, and orange kitchen. As we finished, I asked what time we should be back in the morning to go to synagogue. My father glanced at my mother, then looked at me and said, "Your mother isn't going." We always attended synagogue as a family.

"What do you mean she isn't going?" I said, looking at my mother. She didn't answer or clap back as she usually did. Her eyes were downcast. She said nothing.

"We drove all the way from Toronto to do this as a family and now you aren't going?"

I reacted true to form. I got angry with her. After a few minutes of arguing with no response, I finally gave up and we headed back to the hotel.

The next morning, we returned to their house to pick up my father and go to synagogue. To my surprise, my mother was dressed and ready to go. She looked beautiful, right down to one of the smart hats from her vast collection (as it was a conservative synagogue, married women had to cover their heads, and my mother liked to do that in style). And off we went. Just like that. With no explanation for her bizarre behaviour the night before. As if nothing had happened.

Our seats in synagogue were up on the balcony. As we climbed the stairs, she stumbled and twisted her ankle. At first, I was terrified that she had injured herself, but she was fine. In hindsight, I often found myself wishing that she had broken it. Maybe that would have prevented her from doing what she did.

Following synagogue, we went back to my parents to have leftovers for lunch. We spent the afternoon with them and then headed to dinner at my mother-in-law's. My father-in-law had passed away the previous year.

Michael has a large, loud family. I left the raucous dinner early. I wanted to speak with my parents privately. I needed to try to get control of the situation.

It was only 9:30 p.m., but my parents were already in bed watching TV. They had a queen-size bed, which accommodated my slightly built parents perfectly but always looked tiny to me. I sat opposite them on the divan inherited from my grandma Florence, which my mother had reupholstered in a blue-and-white floral print to match their bedding. I launched into my prepared speech.

"I'm worried. We need to get someone in to help around the house." I then looked directly at my mother and added, "And you need to be on medication." My mother was strangely quiet.

No eye rolling or yelling. She seemed to hear me and take in my words, but she was calm and sedate. Like a dimmer lamp on the lowest setting, barely casting any light. I looked to my father, but he offered no explanation for my mother's strangely placid demeanor.

I continued my "how to get her better" speech until I paused for a moment, hoping for one of them to react. That's when my father said, quietly, "Your mother doesn't want to be here anymore."

Okay. I know what you're thinking. This was not just a sign. This was a warning signal bright enough to get a response from Batman. How could I not see it? But my mother had always generated so much drama that it was impossible to know what was real and what was theatrics.

My father wouldn't make eye contact with me, so I kept talking about cooks and personal support workers and therapy. My mother wasn't fighting me about my plan. I mistook her lack of response for acquiescence. I believed they were finally going to let me step in and help. An unprecedented victory. I could single-handedly fix this! And then I was done talking. It was late. We were all tired. I said goodnight and drove back to the hotel in the dark.

The next morning, we were back at the house to say goodbye. At some point, my father uttered the words that I didn't understand at the time. "See, Rachel?" he said. "Audrey's going to call you when she gets home."

On the drive home, I was delighted with myself for having gotten through to my parents. I was a fucking superhero. Everything was going to be okay.

I can't remember if Lindsay was already in the bedroom with me when Michael told me my parents were dead. Or maybe she sensed that something was wrong and came in. I remember howling like a wounded animal, grabbing onto Lindsay as I collapsed on the floor, losing the towel that was wrapped around me.

I felt like I was watching a scene from a movie shot from above in slow motion. In this continuum of horror, my single biggest regret is Lindsay seeing me like that. It was so ugly and raw. I know she will always carry that with her.

I don't know how long I lay naked on the floor in a state of shock, but I knew that, for Lindsay's sake, I had to try to pull myself together. I got dressed and asked Lindsay to cancel my hair appointment for that morning. I didn't want to inconvenience my stylist.

It was Michael's brother Brad who called to tell him what had happened. Brad and his wife Rosemary lived down the street from my parents. Close friends of theirs lived in the house next door to ours. They called Brad and Rosemary that morning to let them know that there was a swarm of police cars at my parents' house but that they didn't know what had happened. Brad walked over to see what was going on. Ironically, Michael had asked me the previous evening, when I was trying to reach my parents by phone, if he should ask Brad to check on them. For whatever reason, I said no.

When Brad arrived and identified himself, he was told that my parents had died from carbon monoxide poisoning. The car had been running for so long that the gas tank was empty.

Michael was racing home to tell me about my parents and was still on the phone with Brad when he saw my number pop up. Michael didn't want to tell me over the phone but was worried that I had already found out and, if so, he didn't want to ignore my call, so he answered and gave me the news.

I have no idea why, but I called Brad, who was still at my parents' house, and asked to speak to a police officer. I asked the officer if there had to be an autopsy, as I knew from my grandmother's death that would delay the funeral. Ever the efficient planner.

The police officer responded yes, because they had to determine if one had killed the other. Obviously, the officer was absent the day they taught sensitivity training. I knew one thing for certain. One parent had not deliberately harmed the other. I asked him to hand the phone back to Brad.

Brad and I didn't discuss the events of that morning until many years later. At the time, it never occurred to me to ask him what he saw. He had seen my parents through the window. I can't imagine how haunted he must be by that image. He told me that he went into the house. Apparently, the back door was left unlocked. That was a door that locked automatically when it closed, and it was never left open. Did my father rush out when he saw my mother through the garage window and not close the door behind him?

Brad had been in our house before, so he knew my father's office was in the basement. He assumed that if there was a note, that's where it would be. Nothing.

My next call was to Naomi. I was trying to tell her what happened, but I couldn't get the words out. She kept saying she couldn't understand me and finally said she was coming over. Her brother lived ten houses away from my parents. He had also seen the police cars. He called her shortly afterward to tell her what had happened, so by the time she arrived at my house, she knew. I remember her bringing a big bottle of scotch. I thought that was very sensible.

By now, word had started to spread and close friends were descending on my house. Debbie brought over my favourite blintzes from a restaurant called Milk and Honey. They eventually found their way into the freezer where they stayed for years untouched. To this day, I cannot eat a Milk and Honey blintz.

It was the day after Rosh Hashanah and I realized that my aunt Ruthie, who had been in Toronto to be with her daughters Charlotte and Sandi, was likely travelling home to Montreal that day. She would not yet know that her brother was dead.

I had to find her before someone else told her. I called Sandi. She had just dropped her mother off at the train station. Luckily, my aunt was in the business lounge, so Sandi was able to call and tell them to not let her get on the train. Sandi rushed back to the train station. The first thing my aunt said was, "It's Brahm, isn't it?"

Eventually, we started learning more details. The breakfast dishes were still on the table. That meant it probably happened right after we left their house. My mother was still wearing her Nana Banana yellow sweatsuit. The answering machine was unplugged.

We will never know what actually happened, but no one doubts that my mother chose to end her life. That is undisputable. My poor mother, everyone that was close to her accepted that her committing suicide was plausible. But my father? What had happened to him? NO ONE believed that my father had killed himself.

I have since learned that it's quite common for someone who has decided to end their life to become very calm, making peace with their decision. I had read it all wrong. I had mistaken her complacency for agreement. I hadn't realized we crossed way beyond the line from little white lies and obfuscation into dangerous territory. I had seriously misjudged how dire the situation was. Now, incomprehensibly, they were both dead.

The coroner's report that came out a year and a half later said the autopsy showed that my father had a serious heart blockage.

As far as I know, my parents didn't know that. I asked his closest friends, including Max. No one was aware of a heart condition.

In a state of panic and confusion, did he accidentally close the garage door behind him? The carbon monoxide would have been so highly concentrated that he would have been overcome almost immediately. Did he have a heart attack?

OverCat had two events taking place the day my parents died. A Gwen Stefani fragrance launch on a double decker bus in downtown Toronto, and a Playboy fragrance launch in New York. I was supposed to be at the Toronto event in an hour and a half.

Some things are very clear from that day, others a complete blur. I must have called my vice president to tell her what was going on. I also remember getting calls from clients and very bluntly telling them that my parents were dead, and I couldn't talk right now.

Lindsay and Michael went to get Alex from school. He was in gym class and one of his teachers called him out. Alex hates getting into trouble, and he was worried when he saw his teacher. Then he saw the principal and was really worried. When he saw Michael and Lindsay, he knew something bad had happened, but at least he wasn't in trouble.

Being a publicist, I suspected that their deaths would be covered by news outlets, and they were. I prayed for just one thing: no footage of my parents in body bags being wheeled out of the garage. When I did an online search that night, there it was. I didn't know until many years later that Lindsay had also seen the footage. A national news outlet reached out to me a few days later about doing a documentary about my parents. I shut it down.

I don't remember who called the funeral home. I later found out that Naomi was in touch with them and had been instrumental in handling a lot of the details. Michael, Lindsay, Alex, and I flew to Montreal the next day along with Naomi, Sandi, Charlotte, and my aunt Ruthie.

When we got to Montreal, I went straight to the funeral home. Michael tore my parents' house apart looking for a suicide note. He thought that a note would give me some sort of comfort. He never found one. But Lindsay, who was also scouring the house, did find something. On the TV stand in their bedroom was a copy of *The Jewish Book of Mourning*. There was a specific paragraph underlined. This had to have been my mother, she was always underlining passages in books (something that drove me crazy).

The paragraph described what the mourning protocols are if someone passes away between Rosh Hashanah and Yom Kippur (the Jewish day of atonement and the holiest day of the year). From Rosh Hashanah to Yom Kippur, your fate is inscribed and then sealed in the Book of Life. Perhaps that was why my mother was so reticent about going to synagogue? Maybe she knew her name would not be in the book because she was not going to be alive by Yom Kippur.

At the funeral home the first task was to pick out caskets. Not a casket, two caskets. Write the obituary, plan the funeral, prepare for the Shiva. The funeral home was run by two brothers. Normally, they assigned one brother per customer. Not us. For our special clusterfuck, we had both brothers at the meeting.

Just so you know, when you read the word "suddenly" in an obituary, it is often a code word for suicide. I refused to use that word in the obituary. We kept it simple and did not touch on the cause of death.

The next issue was the Shiva. Typically, the mourners come back to the house after the funeral and then you sit Shiva for a week. Because of the Jewish High Holidays, the Shiva would be for a shorter period of time. You don't sit Shiva on the Sabbath or on Jewish holidays. I did not want any Shiva. The thought of people streaming into my parents' house and having to interact with them was something that I just couldn't stomach. In the end, we did two days of Shiva (the day of the funeral and the next day).

I went back to the house after the meeting with the funeral home. How strange to be there without them. The window on the side of the garage was broken, as was the garage door. I didn't stay in the house long, but when I was there, a glass shattered in another room. No one was near it. I looked up and said, "That's not funny, Mom."

Next up, meet with the Rabbi. Rabbi Scheier had a close relationship with my parents, and they were very fond of him. The first question I asked him was about the burial. Technically, in the Jewish religion, suicides are not allowed to be buried on holy ground. He said not to worry about it, which was a relief.

Rabbi Scheier is a very kind man and helped us navigate the trickiness of preparing their eulogy. He did not want to focus on the end of their lives. He wanted to talk about what special people my parents were. But, of course, everybody knew how they died.

The coroner released the bodies (apparently neither had killed the other) and the funeral was set for Sunday, October 5. Naomi's birthday. I wonder if the airlines noticed that hundreds of last-minute flights were booked between Toronto and Montreal.

On Saturday, I had no idea what to do with myself, so Lindsay and I went downtown. We both got blowouts, I bought a pair of black YSL sunglasses to wear to the funeral. I bought Lindsay two dresses at Betsey Johnson. I'm sure this sounds like bizarre behaviour, but we were shell-shocked. It helped distract us from what the next day would bring.

Lindsay stayed glued to my side. When you lose one parent and the other parent is still alive, all the focus is on supporting the remaining parent. But in our case, we had leapfrogged. Suddenly, my sixteen-year-old daughter had become my support system while she was also grieving for two grandparents.

Lindsay has an extraordinary ability to home in on other people's suffering, but whatever teen drama she supported her friends through was negligible compared to this. This could overload anybody's circuits, and she was still a child. A highly intelligent, street-smart child.

I was extremely concerned about both of my kids. In the short-term, how were they going to be able to navigate the funeral and Shiva? It was impossible to imagine that horror. My kids were monitoring me to see how I was holding up. I was doing the same to them. We were all under a microscope.

And what about the longer-term ramifications for them? This was now their trauma to live with. What would their attitudes about suicide be? Would it seep into their consciousness and become an option for them? My mother, as a child, had heard her parents talking about suicide before they were dispatched to the concentration camp. Was that seed always living within her, just waiting for the right time to blossom? I had to protect my children. I wanted to be strong for them. I just wasn't sure I was up to the task.

I didn't sleep the night before the funeral. When it was time to get ready, I put on my Ann Taylor suit. A knee-length skirt with a matching three-quarter length coat. Black wool with white topstitching. Black opaque tights and black patent leather block heel pumps, so that I wouldn't sink into the ground at the cemetery.

Put on your costume, stand where they tell you, recite your lines. I focused on the details because it was impossible to process the reality. There was no way to assimilate their deaths. How do you reconcile that you see your parents one morning, and then they simply evaporate? When I thought about it, trying to make some sort of sense of it all, I always arrived at the same conclusion. It's not possible that this happened. For months after their deaths, I woke up in the morning gasping for breath. Distantly aware in my semi-conscious state that something was very wrong, not yet aware of what it was.

The limousine was meeting us at the house. When I walked into the kitchen, there were eight uniformed staff from the catering company preparing for the Shiva. Naomi arranged everything. What I remember most clearly was the watermelon. It had been cut in half, and they were serrating the edges to make it look pretty. Really? I'm about to bury my parents and what we need is fancy fruit?

And then it was time to go. When the limo pulled up to the funeral home, from behind the safety of the blacked-out window, I could see people from all stages of my life flooding in.

Before the funeral service, the family accepts visitors in a private room. I worried it would be a zoo. It was going to be hard enough to get through the funeral; I didn't want to have to deal with everyone else's grief and pity before it. So, my brother and I made a list of people who were closest to our parents and to us. If you weren't on the list, you didn't get in, like some grotesque VIP party. Someone I had grown up with, who was a member of our synagogue, was stationed at the door monitoring the list.

Lisa, my parents' housekeeper, had been with my parents for decades. I called to tell her what had happened and to give her the funeral details. I told her she should come to the room before the funeral, as I knew she was probably devastated and I wanted to see her. My mother-in-law, however, was not on the list. This did not go over well. "The cleaning lady is allowed in, but I'm not?"

As much as I was in shock, on some level, I felt compelled to try to comfort the people in that room. People who my parents loved. Who I loved. Who loved us. I was very aware that there was an extensive community of people who were in acute pain, but what was there to say? We had all been thrown in the deep end and there was no safe shore to swim to.

We waited in the private room at the funeral home until the "death brothers" told us it was time. Sunglasses firmly in place, I started walking towards the chapel. Just before I left the room, one of the brothers grabbed my arm. "There are a thousand people out there." Literally. He wasn't exaggerating. "Don't look around, just go to your seat." I did as I was told.

The family sits in a special section where everybody can see you. I hated being on display. I already felt like a circus clown. "Oh look, there goes the girl whose parents died together." I felt that this now defined me, just like the Holocaust had defined my mother. People no longer saw me; they just saw tragedy.

The eulogy was delivered by both Rabbi Scheier and Rabbi Shuchat, who had married my parents (he had come out of retirement to officiate). Rabbi Shuchat began talking about the book *Kinderlager*, and how my mother had flown back to Poland to film a documentary. Huh? At first, I wondered if my mother had secretly returned to Poland. I turned to my brother and asked, but he was also unaware of it. I knew that there had been a documentary filmed, but I believed my mother had declined and it was just Tova and Frieda who had participated.

We figured out later that an article about the documentary mistakenly reported that my mother had gone to Poland. I assume this was responsible for the error. Yet another absurd thing in a day where the world had gone awry.

At the cemetery, we had to walk up a hill to get to their graves. I remember that the weather was beautiful. The flowering bushes that dotted the cemetery were still in full bloom. My mother would have liked that. She loved flowers. And then I got to the top of the hill. All I could see was two caskets and a lot of dirt. I couldn't take another step. Dave Yerzy, a close friend for many years, must have noticed. He stretched out his arm and grabbed my hand, guiding me to my place beside the caskets. It is one of the most vivid memories I have of that day.

After the funeral, the house was bursting with visitors. I was standing near the front door. I hadn't cried at the funeral. I didn't cry at the cemetery. But when Miltie and Francy Dines walked though the door, close friends of my parents who now lived in Boston, I collapsed into Francy's arms sobbing. Francy and my mother had trained as nurses together. I couldn't hold back the grief any longer.

And then the questions started. People were actually asking me what happened. It was shocking. But nature abhors a vacuum, so the theories started flooding in. As did the questions.

"There were financial troubles?" No.

"Your father was ill?" Not that I was aware of.

"They were like Romeo and Juliet." Seriously?

"In the end, your mother didn't escape her past. How ironic the way she died." What is wrong with you?

I was not interested in this Family-Feud-style guessing game. Survey says: Who cares. They were dead. There was no prize for the right answer.

People continued to flow in and out of the house. Naomi kept bugging me to eat. I hadn't eaten all day. I had already decided that I wasn't going to eat for twenty-four hours. Why? Why not? I was always the girl who was competing with herself. To be the best dancer in the class. To collect the sales reports faster than anyone else. Now, I was going to be the girl who didn't eat.

As it turned out, I pretty much stopped eating for months. I felt that the pain and discomfort of not eating was appropriate to the situation. If I am not in pain, then I will feel normal and I did NOT want to feel normal. It felt like nothing was ever going to be normal again.

Naomi stood beside me during this tragic receiving line, cringing every time someone hugged me. I do not like being hugged. A fact she knew well.

Ruthie Goldsmith, one of my mother's best friends, captured the absurdity of the situation perfectly. She said that she hoped that my parents were with my grandmother, and that she was giving my mother shit for what she did. I hoped so too.

The Rabbi arrived to do the services. Everyone gathered in the living room. Someone thrust a prayer book into my hands. I did not want to be doing this. Before this happened, I cherished the family time spent during the Jewish holidays. I had loved it as a child and continued the traditions when Michael and I started our own family. Right before my parents' death, I'd recently started going to synagogue more often, enjoying the peacefulness of disconnecting from the outside world for those few hours. But that was over for me now. I didn't blame God. I was just done with religion. If this could happen, what was there left to believe in? The universe had shown its true colours.

I stopped going to synagogue for the High Holidays. Rosh Hashanah dinners and Passover Seders were also banished. We used to celebrate them with my cousins Charlotte and Sandi and their families, but it was too painful now. I tried for a few years but always ended up dissolving in tears. My father had led those dinners, and they were just a reminder that he was gone. Like my mother, celebrations became about who wasn't there.

The next night of Shiva, I refused to participate in the prayers. I sat in the kitchen with a bunch of friends. We were so loud that Michael kept coming into the kitchen to tell us to keep it down. I didn't want to keep it down. I wanted to shriek at the top of my lungs.

I received hundreds of condolence letters, which for some reason, I have kept . . . although I never read them. A month after my parents died, I received a letter from an old friend of my mother's. They had been close but had a falling out, I'm not sure why. In the letter, she wrote that leaving home when I did was the only thing I could have done to save myself. That my mother would have destroyed me if I had stayed.

On the one hand, I did feel that it was true. On the other hand, the comment was such an indictment of my mother. I know the letter came from a good place, but having someone else say it was somehow embarrassing. Like someone spilling our secrets. How many other people thought that too?

I will never know, definitively, what brought my mother to the decision she made. She started seeing a new psychiatrist a few weeks before she died but had only been to two appointments. When I later spoke to him, I asked if he had thought she was suicidal. He said that suicide is always a risk with long-term depression, but no, he had not thought that she was suicidal. Long-term depression? I'd never thought of it in those terms. I just thought that was who my mother was.

During her downward spiral, I'd begged my mother to try anti-depressants. She refused. She told me that the psychiatrist also didn't think she needed them. That never rang true to me. I asked him about that as well. He said he thought that she definitely should have been on medication, but my mother blatantly refused. Since they hadn't yet had time to build trust, he felt it was too soon to push her. He added that if she'd been on medication, this might not have happened.

I am a fighter like my mother, but our battles were different. She fought me like a caged animal my entire life, and she fought her own demons. She fought until she couldn't fight anymore. Then she exited. And that's where our paths split apart.

If my relationship with my mother were a painting, I see her facing me, and you only see me from the back. I am looking at a landscape of utter chaos. She doesn't see it. It's always behind her. My father is standing beside me, also facing my mother, watching helplessly.

My mother lived her life precariously balancing on a pinhead of fear. I tried my hardest to not be ruled by fear. But it was all around me and possibly infiltrated my genes. If you grow up in a household with a mother who's been through hell, her experiences will inevitably bleed into yours. All those decades of my mother's dire warnings, anticipating the bad things that could happen. But now the bad thing had happened. And it was my mother who perpetrated it. If you're "lucky," the trauma walks beside you, a constant companion. And if you're not, it overtakes you.

My mother succumbed. My father was gone. I now felt like I was at great risk. That the trauma would overtake me, too. I was staring over the edge of the precipice and Lindsay was right there teetering beside me.

The house where I grew up.

My maternal grandfather,
Aaron Greenspan.

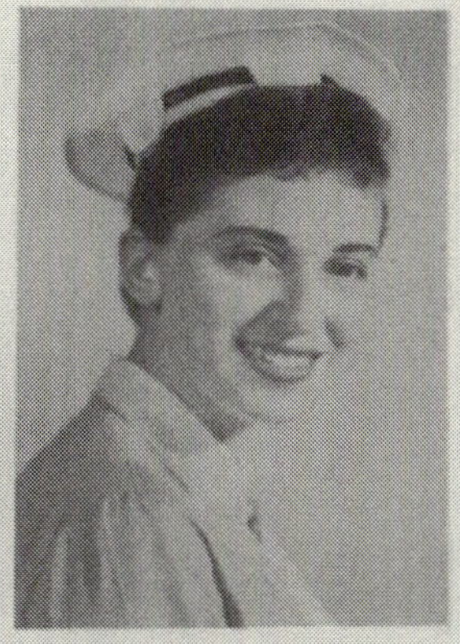

My mom.

My parent's wedding.

My mom in Des Moines, Iowa.

Jack Cymberg, Bubby, my mom, and my dad.

Bubby and me, six weeks old.

My mom before my wedding.

Me and Michael.

Alex and Lindsay.

My mom, me, Lindsay, and Bubby.

My dad with Lindsay.

Bubby, Lindsay, and my mom.

Lindsay, my mom, and Alex.

Lindsay with my mom.

Itzka, my step-grandfather, and Bubby.

Me and Naomi.

Bubby, me, my mom, and Lindsay.

AFTER

Help, I'm Alive

I tremble

They're gonna eat me alive

If I stumble

—Lyrics by Emily Haines, lead singer of Metric

ACCORDING TO THE JEWISH RELIGION, you say mourning prayers for a year. In my twisted state of mind, I created my own game plan. I gave myself a year to tear down my life. To do whatever the fuck I wanted to. I refer to it as my "lost year."

Human beings are cursed with a deep-rooted need to try to make sense of things that can't possibly be explained. Sniffing around the past like a rescue dog in the rubble of an earthquake. Looking for clues and warning signs. I had not yet learned that anything I discovered would never feel like the full story or the right answer. That a tragedy like this would turn even Sherlock Holmes into the world's worst detective.

I was an emotional wreck. I cried every day. And not just in private. No matter where I was. I couldn't control it.

Back in the day, you could smoke on hotel patios. I was having a meeting with a client (and good friend of mine) at the rooftop patio of a fancy hotel. Elliot Page and Drew Barrymore were in town to promote the movie *Whip It*. They were seated directly behind us. I don't remember what set me off, but suddenly, I was sobbing. I have always hoped that they didn't notice. I did, however, make note of the very cute tartan pantsuit Drew was wearing. I think it was Gucci. I tracked down a knock-off a few months later.

I had two goals after my parents died: feel nothing, and lose as much weight as possible. I excelled at both.

What a thrill it was to step on that scale and see that I dropped another pound. I am five foot five, and when I hit 97 pounds, I was exhilarated. It turns out that this was all pretty textbook. Research published in the *Journal of Eating Disorders* revealed that people who have gone through trauma are more likely to engage in disordered eating. Refusing to eat is a way to maintain control when you feel like you have none. It's also a nice way to avoid feeling the feelings, which can be too strong to bear. At 97 pounds, I wore size 00.

I loved the feeling of physically shrinking. Maybe I could even disappear. Then no one could look at me with pity. Or curiosity.

I perfected the recipe for becoming a zombie. Don't sleep and drink a lot.

While my PR agency usually focused on beauty brands and fashion clients, I had accidentally fallen into the music business. My son was playing hockey at an elite level and one of his teammates was the son of a musician who had been part of a very successful Canadian rock band in the eighties. He was putting together a new band, and when he found out I was in PR, he was interested in hiring me. Well, hiring may be a misnomer. I worked for free and ended up paying for a bunch of stuff, including meet and greets with music industry executives. At the time, I was fine with the arrangement. I loved hanging out with the band.

Word got around that I was representing a band, and I was approached by other indie acts. One was a rock trio founded by two best friends who were the driving force of the band. They were twenty-two when I met them. The drummer was thirty-one. I started doing PR for them as well. Then in August, a few months before my parents died, they fired their manager. They sheepishly approached me to take over as their manager. Fuck yeah! That sounded amazing.

Let's call the besties "The Boys." They were lovely young men wholly dedicated to looking like rock stars—mohawks, tattoos, piercings, platinum hair. It's actually a really smart strategy. People don't know who you are, but you must be somebody. They had no record contract and were essentially being supported by their parents, so everything had to be done on the cheap. Unless I paid for it.

Integrating myself into the music industry was not easy. There are so many bands trying to make it. I, of course, believed that despite my complete lack of experience in this area, that under my tutelage, I would propel the band to superstardom. Regular work hours were dedicated to OverCat. Okay, not really. I was there in body but basically floated around the office like an apparition unless I could convince my two senior staff to go out for a boozy lunch or afternoon cocktails.

OverCat was busy, but I was mentally AWOL. A new chapter in my three-ring circus life. Ladies and gentlemen, I invite you to look high above your heads. Watch as Audrey walks the tightrope, somehow balancing crushing grief, demanding clients, and high-profile celebrities, all without a net.

I wanted the world to stop so that I could catch up, but that was, of course, impossible. I had staff to manage. I had clients who, no matter how "understanding" they claimed to be, still expected the work to get done. During this time, one really classy client sent a condolence note which included firing us.

There were three incredible women in my office who picked up the torch and ran with it. I am eternally grateful to them. One left a year later; she wanted out of PR. She was actually planning on leaving much earlier, but she stayed on when my parents died. Another continued rising through the ranks and stayed for ten years. She got scooped up by an international company seven years ago and she's doing great. We still speak and see each other. She is a spectacular human. And then there was the third. We were extremely close, but a few years after my parents died, our relationship soured. It went on for far too long and it ended badly. I'm sure when she thinks of me, if she ever does, there is no love lost there. I, too, am hurt and angry, but I am also able to isolate that year when she was an incredible support both personally and professionally. I can't imagine we will ever forgive each other, but she holds a place in my heart.

Evenings were all about the band. I had a slew of responsibilities, one of which was trying to figure out how to create a revenue stream. There are a lot of clubs that book indie bands, but securing bookings is very difficult. I often stayed at the office until 10 p.m. sending out emails to club venues pitching the band. Even when I was able to book them, these were primarily unpaying gigs. Selling band merch is one way to make money. I designed t-shirts and sweatshirts, had them produced, and set up merch tables at their shows which I would sell from. This was a far cry from my regular life and I loved it.

I fully immersed myself in this new world. I was forty-five but started to dress like I was in my twenties, building a wardrobe of skin-tight mini dresses and platform booties. I got hair extensions down to my waist and became a blonde. This was both time-consuming and expensive. The extensions had to be swapped out every four months or so, and it was an eight-hour process to remove them, dye my hair, and have new extensions put in. All for the low, low price of $1400 a shot. The Boys didn't know my age and I guarded that secret with my life. My charade worked. I was constantly getting carded at the clubs we frequented. The Botox, mermaid hair, and tiny slutty clothes threw everyone off.

I started booking the band in clubs outside of Toronto. This involved loading into an SUV with a trailer full of instruments and speakers hitched up behind. I felt like a chaste groupie. I became obsessed with Pamela Des Barres' memoir *I'm With the Band.* This new lifestyle became a crucial part of my human zombie evolution. When we were out on the road and they were playing gigs, I drank myself into oblivion. When they weren't playing gigs, we went out to clubs to network, and I drank myself into oblivion. We became regulars at a now-defunct club called Tattoo Rock Parlour. There was always a line-up, but the bouncers knew me, so no waiting for us.

One night, I was checking my coat at the same time that a man, who appeared to be at least a decade younger than me, was retrieving his. He was ahead of me but offered to let me go first. We started chatting. He asked me who I was there with. I pointed to my band besties who were in full goth rock star mode. He took at look at them, then turned to me and said, "You're too wild for me." Yes, this married, middle-aged mother of two private school teenagers who lived in a five-bedroom house with a swimming pool had evolved into a creature of the night.

I hung out with The Boys a lot. It was the best way to keep the trauma at bay. I was sleeping about three hours a night. It was perfect. There were frequent road trips to play at music venues several hours away. We would roar down the highway blasting Buckcherry's "Too Drunk to Fuck."

It's difficult for me to face how badly I parented that year. Grief made me oblivious to anyone and everyone. My pain overshadowed my children's needs—familiar territory, one generation later. The kids each had their own way of dealing with the trauma. Alex chooses not to dwell on sad things. But Lindsay was suffering and rebelling.

How disengaged was I? One day, Lindsay told me she had hurt her hand. Looked fine to me—I sent her off to a horseback riding lesson. When the pain persisted, Lindsay took herself to the pediatrician. I got a call from Dr. Gallant telling me that Lindsay's hand was broken, and I had to take her to Sick Kids Hospital immediately. I felt a kind of shame I've never experienced in my life. To this day, I cringe when I look at the photos of Lindsay on her way to her grade eleven formal in a custom-designed gown with a matching ribbon tied around her cast.

Michael was in an impossible position. He wanted to be there for me, but I wasn't there. Years later when I asked him about it, he said he knew how strong I was and that, eventually, I would pull myself out of it.

My family and friends were at a loss as to how to help me. This was compounded by the fact that I had evolved into a human porcupine. If people got too close, my quills ensured that they would be kept at a distance.

Maybe it was our shared history, deep friendship, or the fact that she was a therapist, but Debbie refused to be intimidated by my defensiveness. For months, Debbie continued to show up at my house every Wednesday morning with bagels and cream cheese.

A few months after my parents died, I left a message for the therapist that I had being seeing on and off for a few years. I was currently in an off stage. "My parents died, I would like to come back to therapy."

That message got me an appointment real quick. It's one thing to keep your deepest fears bottled up. It's another to say them out loud. I was terrified of the lesson my kids had learned from their grandmother's suicide. I asked the therapist: "What's the likelihood of someone with suicide in their family killing themselves? Are my kids at risk? Am I?"

My therapist didn't coddle me. "Yes," she said, "there is risk." A South Korean study found that the risk of suicide was three times higher in families that had lost a loved one to suicide than in bereaved families with non-suicide deaths. But then she added that there is no single cause. People who commit suicide are usually dealing with multiple factors such as stresses in their environment, psychological makeup, and a lack of support.

At one of our breakfast sessions, I relayed to Debbie a recent conversation I had with my therapist. It involved big "T" Trauma—a major life event that causes severe distress—and small "t" trauma, a chronic stressor. I looked at Debbie and asked her which one I had. She reached across the table with a smile, grabbed my arm, and said: "Aud, big T. BIG T Trauma." We both laughed. It was so stupid that I was even deliberating which category I fell in to.

My efforts with the band were starting to pay off. At that time, getting radio and video play were the holy grail. One of the biggest radio promoters in Canada was a company called Dale Speaking. The band had been hounding me to connect with Dale. I'd produced a slick circus-themed video for the band complete with a fire eater and snake charmer that we were hoping would get on-air. I sent several emails to Dale with no response. One day, I decided to just pick up the phone, and unbelievably, I got through to him. He agreed to a meeting! On the appointed day, I headed downtown armed with the band's EP. Dale took one listen and said there was no way to get them on the radio. Then I showed him the video. He was interested. He was having a meeting with MuchMusic, Canada's equivalent to MTV, the following week and agreed to pitch it. True to his word, he did, and within two weeks, we were in rotation. We were finally getting somewhere.

And then it all fell apart.

We were playing a show in Winnipeg when I got woken by an early morning phone call from the director of The Boys video. While he was out for drinks the night before with industry people, someone mentioned that The Boys were shopping around for a new manager. They didn't know the director knew me. I was skeptical at first, but when he told me the full story, it was clear that they were. I was numb. I confronted one of The Boys, who denied it. I didn't really believe him.

It was clear that the relationship was heading toward the rocks. In August, a year after I started managing them, I told them I was out. Truthfully, I would have hung on, but the vibes were bad. They had been such a huge part of my life that year and they were truly wonderful people. It was very difficult giving up my rock and roll lifestyle. I stopped staying out all night and seriously cut down on the drinking. I hated giving up my second adolescence and re-entering the adult world. It was a tough transition.

My parents unveiling in Montreal was planned for the labour day long weekend. In the Jewish religion, you unveil the tombstones within a year of death. The timing was terrible for me. The Toronto International Film Festival started a few days later and we were planning a bunch of film premiere parties, but because of other conflicts, that was the only weekend we could do it.

I was dreading the unveiling. I was still in the acute grief phase and just couldn't picture myself back at the cemetery. We made the decision to keep the unveiling private, rather than announcing it publicly, as is usually the case. I was terrified that hundreds of people would attend, and I just couldn't cope with that.

I started getting sick a few days before we were scheduled to go to Montreal. I developed a raging sinus infection. I probably could have forced myself to go but I made the decision to miss it. My body was telling me that I wouldn't be able to handle it and so I listened. Michael went with the kids.

I didn't see my parents' tombstones until 2015 when my dear Uncle Max passed away. He was buried close to my parents, which I somehow found comforting. Maybe they were all together somewhere.

It was almost the one-year anniversary of my parents' death, and I was still not eating, tipping the scale at double digits. One day, I was sitting on the stoop in front of my office smoking, when a lawyer I knew who had an office down the same street walked by. I hadn't seen him since before my parents died. The first words out of his mouth: "You are shockingly thin." Okay, I knew I was thin, but *shockingly* thin? So thin that someone I didn't know all that well felt compelled to say something? It jolted me out of my noneating phase. I started eating again. I was still thin but not "shockingly" so. I never told him about the huge role he played in my recovery, so thank you, Larry.

I still had no ability to concentrate at work. I spoke with my therapist about it, and she suggested EMDR—Eye Movement Desensitization Reprocessing. She explained that it was used to treat trauma and PTSD. Essentially, it involves using side-to-side eye movements to help the brain reprocess and integrate traumatic experiences. After my first session, the therapist warned me to pay attention when I was crossing the street because people tend to be distracted after a treatment. I did it a few times more. I think it was helpful. And I never got hit by a car.

I had been the queen of multitasking, but now I couldn't manage my hamster-wheel life. OverCat landed the Victoria's Secret opening in Canada. This was a VERY BIG deal. There were multiple store launches across the country and we were in overdrive. I was functioning at a very high level, but I was still a mess. I was juggling glamourous assignments, including taking a group of prominent media to the Victoria's Secret Fashion Show in New York. Twitter was just starting to gain traction. I thought social media was a fad. Obviously, it wasn't.

Instead of posting from that trip on Twitter, which is what I should have been doing, I pointed out celebrities to Shinan Govani, a journalist who wrote about celebrities and socialites for a national newspaper. Oh look, there's Adam Levine! Gerard Butler! Carinne Roitfeld! After the show, which Katy Perry performed at, we gathered outside. I was hosting a dinner and then off to the after party.

The party was in full force when we arrived. It was taking place on the main floor of a huge bar. Then I found out that there was a VIP party on the lower level. I assumed because I was with media, that we would have access to the VIP party. Apparently not. I eventually talked my way in and descended the stairs with my guests. Celebrities like Paris Hilton and a bunch of Victoria's Secret angels were ensconced behind a velvet rope. Somehow, I wrangled my way in there as well. People were smoking in that area, so I thought what the hell. I lit up. I was politely escorted out of the area by security. *Note to self, you are not a celeb.*

At that party, I also broke a personal hard and fast rule. My staff are well aware that we DO NOT drink alcohol at events. EVER. But that night, I was all in. And I was sloppy. I bumped into the VP of marketing for Victoria's Secret, and we spoke briefly. Did he know I was drunk? I will never know, but I was so ashamed. It was the one and only time that I ever broke the no alcohol credo.

That hiccup was nothing compared to the biggest professional fiasco of my life. At least so far. I was in New York doing a press event for a fragrance launch that Alexander Skarsgård was the face of. Yes, he is that handsome in person, and he's a lovely man. While I was getting ready for the event in my hotel room, a client called to tell me that an embargoed photograph of another fragrance we were launching had just popped up on Twitter.

In the world of PR, an embargo is when you share information with media, but they are forbidden from going public with it until a specific date. It's always a risk.

Allow me to take you through the perfect storm of what happened. My longest client relationship was with a company that was doing huge celebrity fragrance deals. By longest, I mean that I had been consulting with them for eighteen years at this point. The women I worked with were not just clients. We also shared deep personal relationships.

The company announced a fragrance deal with Lady Gaga. I love Lady Gaga and I am a dedicated "little monster." It was a career high to be working on this campaign. The launch planning was in the works for months. We had previewed the fragrance and the bottle to a select group of media a few months prior to the launch date. They were aware of the embargo dates and had to sign nondisclosure agreements (NDAs). Because print magazines have much longer lead times than digital media, this was standard operating procedure.

There was a global launch strategy planned. The fragrance, which would only be sold in one major department store location in cities across the world, would launch at the same time regardless of the time zone. Usually, when you have a high-profile fragrance launch, it is carried in multiple stores in the same city which makes sense. You want it to be available to as many consumers as possible. This launch was defying that strategy. The thinking was that Lady Gaga is so huge, people would flock to that one store and wait for hours to get their hands on the fragrance.

We had dozens of meetings with the department store that we were launching with in Canada, and were well down the road on the concept, which included a huge media event, consumer events, and spectacular window displays. In PR parlance, this is known as a "take over."

A few weeks after the initial media preview where the embargoes were signed, a journalist from one of the magazines who was unable to attend the event asked for an unrelated fragrance to be sent to her. Because she had missed the event, my client asked that we send her the Lady Gaga fragrance as well. Storm clouds are gathering.

The OverCat team member who sent the fragrance to the journalist did not ask her to sign an NDA. That's the protocol. Get a signed NDA, then send the fragrance to the journalist. It was a mistake. We should have never sent her the Lady Gaga fragrance without having her sign the NDA first. The journalist had no way of knowing that she should not post about the fragrance. Clouds are getting darker.

Which brings me to that hotel room in New York. The client calls to tell me that the journalist posted a picture of the fragrance on Twitter. It is important to note that we were in the very early days of social media and did not yet understand the power it could yield. I asked if the picture had been taken down. It had. I reassured the client that we should be fine. We were light years away from fine. What I didn't realize at the time was the picture had already been shared, so even though the original post was down, the picture was out there. It went viral. BOOM! The storm breaks.

Everyone was furious. The Canadian division of the company, the company's head office, and Lady Gaga. We were fielding media inquiries from around the world. It proved to be so catastrophic that the global events that had been planned were scrapped. Luckily, another market had a major fuck up that took the focus away from us. They hosted an unsanctioned event with a Lady Gaga impersonator. Big no-no. Huge. The company decided to cancel all global events to support the launch.

This was the beginning of the end of our relationship with the client. A new management team came in and immediately issued a Request for Proposals (RFP). Although we were invited to participate as the incumbent agency, it became obvious at the pitch meeting that we were dead in the water.

I should have been paying better attention. As the agency owner, I am ultimately responsible. The buck stops with me. And it did.

Even though I knew we were likely going to lose the account, I was devastated when it happened. I loved the people I worked with. I loved flying around the world to high-profile celebrity events. From a financial perspective, they were very important to our bottom line. On top of that, they were a huge source of self-esteem. I was forced to realize that I had been looking for love in all the wrong places. A client's love is fickle. No matter how hard you work, no matter how great your results are, they will break up with you at some point.

I did not just drop the ball. I literally handed it over to our competition. It was a teachable moment. Seeking validation from the outside world is a bottomless pit. What really matters is how the people who love you see you. And most importantly, how you see yourself. To find the strands that make you believe in you.

It took me years to tune back into my business. Networking is a huge part of staying relevant. I couldn't bear to do it anymore. Social media continued to gain traction. I continued to mostly ignore it. In client pitches, I was asked about my social media numbers, which were abysmal. We lost a lot of those pitches. This was new for me. If I got into a room with potential clients, I usually won the business. Now I wasn't.

My Dad

THE BIGGEST UPSIDE OF THE "LOST YEAR" was that I was able to banish my parents from my thoughts. I was so successful at it that I added another fourteen years just for good measure. When I found them creeping in, I visualized physically pushing them away. Ironically, in life, it was my mother who dominated my existence. But in death, it was my father.

He came from a "good family." Both his parents' families had been in Canada for several generations, having immigrated from Eastern Europe. His father Ben was the first Jewish orthodontist in Montreal. His mother Florence wasn't a particularly warm person, and after he married my mother, he formed a special relationship with Bubby. I think that my mother was jealous of their relationship because Bubby rarely criticized him.

Growing up, my father was a skinny, funny-looking kid who was bullied at his public school for being Jewish. Exceptionally intelligent, he earned an Honours degree in math and physics before attending medical school. He was goal-oriented and had tremendous inner strength, but it was his kindness to others that was his most remarkable trait.

When Naomi's father died unexpectedly at fifty-five, my father would take her mother, Roselle, to the symphony. Friends and relatives would call frequently to solicit medical advice. He never resented the interruption.

My father was a doppelgänger of Larry David. Unlike my mother, he had no fashion sense. Plaid shirts worn with striped pants were not an unusual combo for him. It was a great source of family amusement.

He loved music and his voice would fill the house when he sang along to the records he played in our main floor den. One of his favourite songs was "Bridge Over Troubled Water" by Simon and Garfunkel. To this day, I change the radio station whenever that song comes on. It's just too painful. My father was the bridge over troubled water.

My father saved my life. He was my "Moonbase Alpha." If you don't get the reference, Moonbase Alpha was the space station on the television show *Space: 1999*. The production values were horrible, but it was a Hyams family favourite.

In our family, I saw myself as the expendable technician sent out to fix whatever was wrong with the spacecraft. Tethered to the ship but at a constant risk of running out of oxygen or being squished by space debris. It was my father who always reeled me in. He always looked at me with wonder. As if he couldn't believe I existed and was from a part of him. It was a sharp contrast to how I saw myself reflected in my mother's eyes.

My father attended medical conferences several times a year and always came home with a gift. I was more excited about the gift than him coming home. After one trip, he presented me with a stuffed Babar the Elephant. I thought it was a horrible gift and let him know it. I was such a spoiled brat. Over the years, I came to love Babar. He came with me when I left for university and is the only stuffed animal I have kept from my childhood. His bowler hat is long gone and the beautifully tailored green suit is moth-eaten, but he stands on a window ledge in the basement of my home. I pass him twice a day when I go downstairs to feed the cats. It breaks my heart every time.

My mother had a lot of rules. My father was easy-going. He stood up for me, often incurring my mother's wrath.

At eight years old, I started badgering my parents to get a pet, preferably a kitten or a puppy. My mother adamantly refused. She didn't like animals. Also, she was convinced, despite my promise that I would take full responsibility for this hypothetical pet, she would become the primary caregiver. It was my father who eventually brokered a compromise. We got two turtles. We named them Sunday and Monday. They were dead within weeks.

Next up—fish. My father and I went to the pet store and bought ten fish, mostly neons, and a tank to house them. The tank came unassembled, and my father proved to be spectacularly inept at putting it together. After five hours, he was still struggling. It was a Saturday night and my parents had plans to go out. My mother kept poking her head into my bedroom, asking when he was going to be done. She finally declared that she wasn't waiting any longer and that they needed to leave. The fish tank appeared to be in good shape when they left.

The next morning, I woke up to dead fish scattered all over my desk. We hadn't realized that we had to put a lid on the aquarium to prevent them from leaping out. He felt horrible.

The time I cherished the most with my dad was going to the movies. It started with Woody Allen comedies, because my mother didn't like them but my father was a huge fan. The first one we saw was *Take the Money and Run*. I was too young to understand a thing about the movie, but it didn't matter. I was there with my dad.

He later took me to *Jesus Christ Superstar* because I had, somehow, become obsessed with seeing it. We also went to see *Tommy* when I was twelve. Probably somewhat inappropriate for my age, but my parents never censored anything.

This lack of censorship led to a few uncomfortable moments. On a family vacation in Plattsburgh, New York, when I was fourteen, we went to see *Saturday Night Fever*. I loved the soundtrack and had a huge crush on John Travolta. My mother was concerned it wasn't age-appropriate, but my father didn't see it as an issue. Everything was going fine until John Travolta, as Tony Manero, utters, "Hey, you assholes almost broke my pussy finger." Sitting there in the dark, I'm sure my parents were just as mortified as I was.

We shared a great love of cats. When I moved to Toronto, one of the first things I did was adopt two cats. At one point, I had five.

It was my father who provided me with the most valuable life lessons. When I complained that I felt underappreciated at work, he was my cheerleader. He told me I was a smart girl with good instincts. He encouraged me to listen to my gut. He taught me that if you work hard, eventually, people will notice. He said that I could do anything I set my mind to. I listened. He was right.

When I was very pregnant with Lindsay, my father came on his own to visit me. He had never done that before. Our lives were about to profoundly change, and I think he just wanted to spend some time with his little girl before that happened. It had been a very long time since we had been just the two of us. I think about that visit a lot. Just me and my dad, making me feel special and loved.

Once I had children, my parents made the drive to Toronto often. I think it was an added bonus for my father that he got to spend time with the cats. He particularly bonded with a silver tabby named Millie who only liked me and my dad.

When Michael was travelling overseas for work, I couldn't stand just sitting around the house with the kids, so we went on adventures. One day, when we returned from a trip to the zoo, I couldn't find Millie. After much searching, I discovered her in a nook in the basement. Her back legs were paralyzed. It was nine o'clock at night, but I loaded my seven-year-old and five-year-old kids into the car and rushed to the emergency vet. Millie had a blood clot and couldn't be saved. The receptionist supervised the kids while I stayed with Millie as she was put down.

I was a total mess. Losing a pet is completely devastating to me. It always sends me into a tailspin. In the car on the way home without Millie, I was sobbing as I drove, the kids buckled in the back seat. Suddenly, Alex, in his sweet little boy voice, says, "Don't cry, Mummy, we can go back and get her tomorrow." Lindsay explained to him that Millie was not coming home. I cried harder.

I called my dad in the morning to tell him what had happened. I knew he would be the only one who could understand my depth of grief. A few days later, I received a condolence letter from him. My father was such a compassionate person. Maybe too compassionate. Can you be too compassionate? It interfered with his ability to be a surgeon. It trapped him in my mother's web.

My father had a deep-rooted sense of obligation to others. His mother developed Alzheimer's at age seventy-five and lived to be ninety-seven. He visited her every week, even though she had no idea who he was.

When his sister's husband Raymond had a massive coronary and was in the ICU at the hospital where he worked, he was a constant presence. After Raymond passed away, he spent a lot of time with his sister helping her navigate her grief.

Once he had grandchildren, he spent countless hours driving back and forth from Montreal to Toronto to celebrate birthdays, attend dance recitals, and watch school plays.

When my mother started spiralling, I felt my father starting to slip away. He was frustrated with me and wanted me to be nicer to my mother. I knew things were bad. I just didn't know how bad. I guess he was hoping that if my relationship with my mother was better, that maybe she would bounce back.

Despite this new dynamic between us, I loved my father dearly. He had achieved the highest accolade that any parent can. He had filled my toolbox with survival skills. He made me feel loved just as I was.

My father was eternally optimistic. Or maybe it was willful blindness. I think he thought that if he just tried harder, he could cure my mother. Make up for everything she had lost. He built her a beautiful life, but it was not enough. After my parents died, my Aunt Ruthie told me that my father had always been attracted to "broken bird" girlfriends. It didn't surprise me. I think that's one of the things that attracted him to medicine. He was trying to fix the world.

The thought had occurred to me several times in the last year of his life that my mother would eventually kill my father. Not literally, but through a sustained campaign of anxiety, fury, and need. I never imagined that she would actually be involved in his death.

In the end, he was collateral damage.

Lindsay

WHILE I WAS STILL WANDERING THROUGH THE FOG of my lost year, Lindsay was applying to universities. She did all her applications with her guidance counsellor at school. I didn't even know where she was applying until she announced she was accepted into the film program at Concordia University. Concordia was in Montreal.

The previous summer, Lindsay trained at The Joffrey Ballet School in New York and had been offered a year-long internship. I was desperate for her to take it, but it was my dream, not hers. She pointed out that since she was the one who would be taking class eight hours a day, it was her decision. Fair enough. I joked that maybe The Joffrey wouldn't notice if I took her place instead.

I knew she would go away to school, but I did not want her to be in Montreal and told her so. For me, it was the epicentre of my pain, but Lindsay felt a tremendous pull to be there, and, on some level, I understood that. How ironic. My mother didn't want me to move to Toronto. I didn't want Lindsay to move to Montreal.

Before my parents died, Montreal was a place of joy for Lindsay. When she was a baby, Michael and I drove to Montreal frequently to visit both sets of grandparents and the slew of first cousins on Michael's side.

From the time she was born, Lindsay and my mother had a special relationship. She was my parents' first grandchild and soaked up all the attention that went along with that. Lindsay was a willing participant in all the things her Nana wanted to share with her—knitting, baking, going on excursions.

Their favourite outing was the "flower show," a greenhouse down the street from my parents' house that I had also loved as a child. When you first walk in, there is an explosion of bright flowers and a heavy, humid, lush fragrance. At Easter, they would bring in live bunnies to frolic in the foliage. Crossing over a small bridge led to an indoor goldfish pond, where she threw in pennies and made wishes. Sometimes when I'm in Montreal and feeling particularly sad, I go there and weep.

Even as a child, Lindsay always kept her cards close to the vest. Alex was more of an open book but Lindsay, like me, kept a lot of things hidden. I usually had a sense for when she was in trouble. I just never knew at the time exactly what that trouble was.

In grade four, she began having issues handing in her schoolwork on time, to the point where I was asked to come in and discuss it with her teacher.

Lindsay was extremely creative about giving plausible reasons why she was unable to hand in her work, and for a while, her teachers let it ride. At the tense parent-teacher interview, when they flagged this as a real concern, I was defensive. I was not interested in what I took as criticism of my perfect daughter. I jokingly told her teacher that she should remember this discussion when Lindsay won an Academy Award. The teacher was not amused.

This problem persisted into high school. The same thing would happen year after year. She was fine with tests, but essays always resulted in missed deadlines, tears (Lindsay), and yelling (me).

Clearly, Lindsay wasn't able to get the situation under control herself, so she agreed to see a therapist. After a few sessions, we met with her therapist. She thought it was possible that Lindsay had ADD. I was incensed. Everyone was getting diagnosed with ADD. They were just going to throw a label on her and possibly prescribe medication. I refused to accept the diagnosis. We didn't have her officially tested. We didn't even tell her what the therapist had said. The school year ended, so no more therapy.

I deeply regret how I handled the situation. I made it about me. Not about what Lindsay needed. My beautiful, bright, engaging, captivating daughter could not have ADD. But she does. And I forced her to struggle with it on her own. I needlessly subjected her to anxiety around her ADD because I refused to consider it.

Lindsay has since taken the initiative to deal with it herself. As her career evolves into management positions, she is proactively addressing it. Lindsay and I have discussed her ADD at length. While it can be challenging to navigate, she also feels that it is a "superpower" that allows her to excel at work. She is the queen of multitasking.

Like her mother before her, high school for Lindsay was ten percent academics, ninety percent social life. As a former wild child, I knew what I was potentially in for. We had frank discussions with both kids about drugs, drinking, and sex. We let them know that they could talk to us about anything, and they would not get in trouble for doing so.

I was delighted that fifteen-year-old Lindsay did not seem to have inherited my party girl ways. I have since been disabused of that notion. I knew that she and her friends weren't angels, but I had no inkling what was really going on.

For her sixteenth birthday, Michael and I threw her a lavish party in a cool industrial space. The Boys played live. We had a DJ. It was fully catered, complete with a chocolate fountain. Lindsay wore a custom replica of a spectacular Miu Miu outfit. I wore a sequin mini dress with thigh-high stiletto suede boots. One of Lindsay's friends asked if I was with the band. This was the party that my parents bailed on at the last minute.

I had several conversations with Lindsay prior to the party about not wanting alcohol snuck in. Lindsay was one of the eldest in her grade, so most of the kids were still fifteen. She told me "she heard me." Years later, she revealed that her friends hid vodka bottles in the toilet tanks in the women's washroom, and they had all been wasted. Okay, points for ingenuity.

A few months after my parents died, I learned, through a friend (who heard it from her daughter) that Lindsay was doing MDMA (ecstasy or molly). I didn't even know what that was. When I confronted Lindsay, she told me she had tried it a few times but didn't do it anymore (that was not true). A week later, I found a bag of weed in the washing machine. She forgot to take it out before putting her jeans in the laundry. I made a big deal about it. She didn't seem to care. She was more concerned that her weed was ruined.

When it came time for Lindsay to move to Montreal, I went with her and set up her apartment. There was no drama. She was so excited, and I did not want to take away from that.

During her first week in Montreal, Lindsay got "Be at Peace" tattooed on her ribs. She says she felt compelled to do it in memory of her grandparents. She knew how much I hated tattoos. To me, they echoed my mother and grandmother's Auschwitz branding. So, she hid it from me.

At least once a year, Lindsay and I took Caribbean beach vacations, and she went to great lengths to make sure I didn't see it. When she finally showed it to me, eighteen months after she got it done, I understood. It was an acknowledgement of her grief. She also prepared me for the fact that she was going to continue getting tattoos. Which she has. A LOT of them. Including a line that runs down the entire length of her body, which she jokes is what holds her together.

Lindsay seemed to be doing great in Montreal. She has always been susceptible to strep throat and had two serious bouts when she was there. I received a call from her while I was at work that she was in the emergency department. She developed a strep-related abscess on her tonsils and needed to have it drained.

I raced to the airport, but there was an ice storm in Montreal and all flights were grounded. Trains were still running, so I beelined it to the station. It took me so long to get to Montreal that the procedure was done before I could get there. She was back at her apartment when I arrived. She had four roommates, so I decided to take her to a hotel to recuperate.

Her throat was so raw and swollen that she basically couldn't eat, so I bought her a small tub of ice cream. I was trying to scoop some into a bowl for her, but it was frozen solid so that when I tried to pry a small amount free the entire contents came flying out and landed on the hotel carpet. We looked at it, looked at each other, and both burst out laughing.

The second bout of strep required more serious intervention. She told me she visited a walk-in clinic and they'd prescribed antibiotics. We had been down this road before and usually after forty-eight hours, she was on the road to recovery, but not this time. She was still symptomatic, and her fever wouldn't break. I told her I was going to come to Montreal. She insisted I didn't. On day four of her illness, I informed her what time I would be arriving.

I was concerned that we were dealing with antibiotic-resistant strep and took her to a hospital emergency room. They were concerned too. She was admitted and put on IV antibiotics.

As part of the admission process, they needed to ask her about drug use and sexual history. I got up to leave so that she could have privacy, but she told me it was fine to stay. She provided a detailed report about a myriad of sexual partners, cocaine, and recreational Adderall use. I sat there in stunned silence. I had no idea that the money we were giving her was being used to buy coke.

Her fever finally broke, and she was released from the hospital. I asked her about the drug use, and she reassured me she was fine. She was doing well in school, she seemed happy. I chose to believe it.

We didn't have a meaningful conversation about what I learned that night until years later, when I finally brought up the topic. I was curious if my parents' death had been a catalyst for her drug use.

She shared with me that before they died, she would occasionally smoke weed with her friends. There was a lot of coke around then too, but she wasn't interested. After they died, she thought, *Why the fuck not?*

During that frank conversation, Lindsay also told me that she and her high school friends started hitting the bars when she was sixteen. As it turned out, these were the same bars I was frequenting with The Boys during my lost year. She told me that before she went out, she always checked which bar I was going to, so I didn't accidentally run into her.

Lindsay switched out of Concordia into a fashion management program at Lasalle College. After she graduated, she moved back to Toronto.

That was when she made the decision to stop doing coke. She felt it was becoming a problem. She considers herself in recovery. I, of course, blame myself.

Turns out I was missing the boat on a number of things about how Lindsay was coping. As I mentioned, the Jewish High Holidays always lay me low. For some inexplicable reason, the depth of sadness varies from year to year. I never realized, although I should have, that Lindsay was experiencing the same syndrome.

Lindsay and I had never really discussed my parents. We all just moved on as best we could. I thought if she wanted to bring it up with me, she would have, but I was wrong.

Ten years after my parents died, Lindsay was having one of her more difficult High Holiday reactions. She approached Michael and shared that she was having a really tough time. Michael sat me down. He told me Lindsay was struggling. She wanted to talk to me about my parents but hadn't because she didn't want to upset me.

I was stunned. I called her immediately and told her I would talk to her about anything she wanted to. I apologized for making her think that she couldn't. From that day on, we speak openly about my parents. Most times, those conversations end up with both of us in tears, but that's okay. It's part of the ongoing process.

I asked her if she felt I was too overprotective when she was growing up. She said, "Yes, until Nana and Poppa died, and then you didn't give a shit." Out of the mouths of babes.

You would think that after having been raised by a mother who had a life plan for me, which I rejected, that I would not do the same to Lindsay. But I did. I wanted her to fall in love with the perfect man—kind, handsome, good job. To get married. To provide me with my much-longed-for grandchildren.

Lindsay dated a series of men I considered NSFM (not suitable for marriage). As it turns out, that's not an issue. She doesn't want to get married. She has made the decision to not have children. She has her own valid reasons for that choice. I worry it is an indictment of my parenting. She assures me it is not.

My father instilled me with a strong work ethic. His legacy extends to Lindsay. She was working a series of hospitality jobs when, she told me one day while we were out grocery shopping in December, that she had decided to do a three-year paralegal program. She had registered to start in January. I was thrilled! She joked that it was my Chanukah present.

COVID hit during her first semester, and everything went online. It was challenging for her to learn this way, but she completed it. She was also working three jobs. Even though we offered to support her while she was in school, she wanted to do it on her own.

Following the completion of her program, she was required to do a paralegal placement and write a licensing exam. Then she was offered a management position in one of the nightclubs she was working at. She thought I would be upset that she wanted to take the job. I wasn't. By that point, I accepted and respected that Lindsay had to make her own life choices. She has excelled at her job, even though working in a nightclub necessitates a vampire-like existence.

She continues to get tattoos and dye her hair wild colours (currently violet). She told us she is pansexual. She believes love comes in many shapes and sizes and wants to be open to that. I think that is a beautiful way to look at the world.

We still take our annual vacations. On a recent trip, I booked us a house in Palm Springs. When we got there, I asked her which of the three bedrooms she wanted. She said, "You mean we aren't going to share a room?" I do not take for granted that my thirty-three-year-old daughter still wants to take trips with me. That we can spend 24/7 together and enjoy each other's company.

Lindsay has worked very hard to become the person that she wants to be, and she is spectacular. She is a wonderful daughter and friend. She is a hard worker. She cares about her community. And now, she and I have a relationship built on love and mutual respect rather than obligation and guilt. I am grateful that I have a degree of self-control that my mother did not have. It has allowed me to have the kind of relationship with my daughter that my mother so desperately craved—and ultimately failed—to have with me. What more could a parent hope for?

Filling the Hollow

I HAVE BEEN GOING TO A VARIETY OF THERAPISTS since I was twenty-eight years old. Therapists are like boyfriends; you need to find the right one for you. My feelings about therapy have evolved over the years. At first, I was terrified. I didn't know what to expect and my mother had fought like a steer to avoid therapy, so that wasn't a ringing endorsement.

My first therapist's office was on the third floor of her house. I was embarrassed that I was in therapy. At that point, I didn't look at it like I was making a brave decision to help myself. I viewed it as a sign of weakness. I didn't want to be in someone's home. I wanted an anonymous office. I thought it would be like what I saw in TV and movies. I wait in a room, and the previous patient exits from a back door, so I never see them, and they never see me. I had too much anxiety about going and only lasted a few weeks.

The second therapist's office was also in his home, but thankfully there was a private entrance into his basement office for patients. This was much better for me. He was excellent. At that time, I was primarily dealing with trying to navigate new motherhood, running a business, and having some semblance of a life outside of that. He was very practical, and solution-driven, which I could relate to. His best advice was that I apply the strategic approach I used in business to my personal life. Solve the problem. Don't freak out about it. A few months after we started, he accepted a teaching position outside of Toronto. I'd come to rely on him and took our breakup badly. To this day, I google him occasionally to see if he still lives out of town.

I decided that I would try to handle things on my own. I couldn't bear to go through my history again with another therapist. On the upside, therapy had given me a new level of introspection. In my early thirties, I realized that a feeling that I had been carrying around since I was an adolescent, had never abated. I call it The Hollow. I feel that, at the core of my being, there is a void that nothing can fill. And I have tried.

Boys, a busy social life, becoming a wife and mother, buying and flipping houses, a career on steroids. Shopping is my biggest Hollow antidote. When I feel badly about myself, which is fairly often, I buy clothes or shoes or bags. I know that no amount of pink vintage Chanel jackets or Alexander McQueen steel-toed combat boots will make up for the emotional vacancy sign blinking in my soul. But I love the momentary high. Michael and I have flipped five houses over the years. Most people are concerned about kitchens and bathrooms. We focus on closet space. In our previous house, Michael built me a walk-in closet that filled an entire spare bedroom. In our newest house, my collection occupies six large closets.

Has it worked? Nope. Still there. Maybe I inherited it? Maybe my chaotic childhood caused it? Regardless, I acknowledge that it isn't going anywhere.

Over the years, I've added names to other issues I've been dealing with.

Interestingly, it was Lindsay, not a therapist, who suggested that I have Body Dysmorphic Disorder. One day, we were trying on clothes in front of the full-length mirror in my closet and I was complaining that I looked fat. "You have BDD," she said. I didn't know what that was. Once she explained it, I realized, of course I do. That's why five-year-old me thought my legs looked fat in ankle socks. That's why, when I look in a mirror, I see bulging thighs. Why I am more reliant on a number on a scale than trusting my reflection in a mirror.

I had been out of therapy for about ten years when I decided to see therapist number three. I was still not comfortable in my own skin. Unable to be present or happy in the moment. I saw her for many years. I developed a routine. Every Tuesday morning, I had a blowout at 9 a.m., followed by a therapist appointment at 10 a.m. Eventually, I felt like I was stagnating. Therapy had just become bitch sessions. So, I ditched therapy and kept the blowout.

This was the therapist I returned to after my parents died. At that point, I wasn't willing to do a deep dive about my relationship with my mother. I was not in a good head space, and thought that maybe I should try medication. The dark clouds just wouldn't lift. It was not easy for me to ask my therapist her thoughts about me going on medication. She wasn't a psychiatrist so she would not have been able to prescribe it, but I felt she was the best person to assess the situation.

As soon as I mentioned medication, she said she didn't think I needed it. It must have been the shocked expression on my face that made her do a 360. I felt she was covering her tracks when she started asking if I felt I needed it. But the trust was broken.

I continued therapy for a few more months but found myself getting angry before every appointment about stupid things. I couldn't find a parking spot. Why did I have to take my winter boots off at the door? It had stopped working for me. It's difficult to tell a therapist that you no longer want to continue. She was gracious. I was relieved. Then I was on my own again. I didn't pursue the medication option.

And then on Friday, March 13, 2020, the world changed. The drumbeat of COVID had already started to affect OverCat. Earlier in the week, we decided to cancel all our upcoming client events for the next month. That afternoon, I went out, bought pastries for the staff, and opened a bottle of Prosecco. We joked about the situation. I told everyone to work from home for the next two weeks.

By Monday, we were in catastrophe mode. My inbox was flooded with client emails featuring the subject line "Can We Chat?" I am well acquainted with the "can we chat?" phrase, and it very rarely means something good. Everyone was in a panic, which was understandable. In those early days, we didn't even know if humanity would survive. Client call after client call let me know that we were on an indefinite freeze. In a flash, my business was teetering. I sat in my backyard smoking and sobbing, watching everything I had built crumble. I had payroll to meet. I leased an expensive office. I had a mortgage. How was I going to stay afloat?

There were a few clients that stayed on and needed help navigating their businesses through COVID. OverCat staff who were on contract did not get renewed. I negotiated with my landlord on rent. Somehow, we made it through.

I was used to going to the office everyday and working long hours. I travelled a lot. Now, I was landlocked at home. I became terrified that with constant access to my kitchen, I would eat all the time and gain weight, so I cut my daily food consumption in half. Once again, the pounds came flying off. An upside to the pandemic!

When we were in lockdown, I started taking long walks with Debbie. After our first outing, as we stopped in front of her house, Debbie said to me, "I think you have dysthymia, and that you should consider being on medication." I had no idea what dysthymia was. She explained that it was long-term, low-level depression. I was stunned. What on earth had I said on that walk to make her think that? Debbie is a therapist; she had known me since we were sixteen, and she is not one to throw around a diagnosis carelessly.

Was I a functioning depressive? I had never thought of myself as depressed. I just thought I had a very negative view of the world. More cynical than clinical. Sure, sometimes I get sad for prolonged periods of time and have to pull myself out of it, but don't most people grapple with that? I was always able to perform at a high level. I didn't retreat to the bedroom like my mother did.

Initially, I didn't tell anyone what Debbie had said to me. I needed to process it. The more I thought about it, the more it seemed possible. Was this The Hollow I had been carrying around for decades?

Alex was always accusing me of focusing on doom and gloom. Armed with the knowledge of my diagnosis, I proudly told him, "See, I have dysthymia, it's not that I just have a negative view of the world."

Alex looked at me and said, "Okay, and you aren't going to do anything about it?" And he was right. I was using it as a rationalization when really, it should be the impetus to do something.

I had been pulling myself out of these "low points" in my life for decades, but now I realized there was an alternative. I called my GP and told her I wanted to consider taking anti-anxiety and depression medication. It was the height of COVID. I'm sure many people were jumping on the medication bandwagon. She asked me why, and I told her. She ordered bloodwork just to make sure there wasn't something physical going on. When the results came back with an all clear, she put me on a low-level dose. It can take up to six weeks for the medication to kick in but by week two, I noticed a huge change. The highs and lows evened out. In a strange way, I found I couldn't even access them, which was a good thing.

This clarity also made me realize that there were likely a few other things in play. I had long suspected I had ADD. Maybe that's why I reacted so negatively to Lindsay's diagnosis. It was an indictment of me. I had passed it onto her.

I do find it challenging to focus on a task that requires intense concentration. I go through a series of mental gymnastics to make myself sit the fuck down. But like Lindsay, I see an upside to it. I am an effortless multitasker. I don't become overwhelmed. It is my superpower, too.

One day, while scrolling through my phone, I was drawn into a clickbait sponsored post. It was for Global English Editing, whatever that is, written by Isabelle Chase.

In large bold font, the headline read: If you double-check if the door is locked (even when you know it is), psychology says you likely have these 8 distinct traits.

Yup, that's me. So, I followed down the rabbit hole.

You value safety above everything. You crave security—physical, emotional, and psychological. *Check.*

You're detail-oriented by nature. *Check.*

You embrace personal responsibility. *Check.*

You have a hint of perfectionism. *Check.*

You practice mindfulness (even if you don't realize it). The act of verifying can actually be a moment of awareness—one where you stop, pause, and ground yourself. *Check.*

You're highly empathetic to others' fears—You sense how others might worry and try to ease that concern before it even has a chance to surface. *Check.*

You hold lingering worries but want to manage them—quieting a tiny voice that says, "What if you're wrong?" These voices can pop up in different areas of life: finances, job decisions, or personal relationships. You're not paralyzed by these worries, but you do prefer to keep them in check. *Check.*

You believe in practical rituals of the mind. Rituals can be powerful. They give structure, comfort, and predictability to our lives. Double-checking is a mini ritual: a consistent action that signals "all is well" to your brain. *Check.*

So, there was an explanation for why I had to line up my stuffed animals in the exact order every night when I was a child! Why the shampoo bottles had to be arranged a certain way. I was trying to calm a restless mind that believed if I didn't do these things, something bad would happen to the people I loved.

I decided that it was probably a good idea to start therapy again in conjunction with the medication. During COVID, therapists were swamped but Debbie pulled in a favour from a psychiatrist she knew. As soon as the therapist learned that I was the child of a Holocaust survivor, that's all she wanted to focus on. She felt that the only way to move forward was to excavate the past. She was an excellent therapist, but that was not where my head was at. I wanted to focus on moving forward. We parted ways and I put my name on a waiting list for a Cognitive Behaviour Therapist (CBT).

It took a few months, but I was finally sent a very in-depth intake form to fill out. This was still during COVID, so all appointments were virtual. I found that awkward but didn't have a choice. The first two appointments focused on the intake form and what my objectives were for therapy. On the third appointment, she told me that she thought I had a serious eating disorder and presented me with two options. Switch to a therapist who specializes in eating disorders or bring my GP into the conversation. I was stunned. Yes, I know I am overly concerned about my weight. No, I do not have a severe eating disorder. I ended the session early. Paid what I owed and wrote her a scathing email. I was on my own again and now gun shy about therapy.

Once I started writing the book, I thought it was a good idea to revisit therapy. Lindsay went to a practice with multiple therapists that she highly recommended. I filled out their online form and set up a phone appointment to see who I would potentially be a good fit with. Obviously, I could not see Lindsay's therapist. I was offered two options. Both seemed excellent. I chose the clinic director. Bring in the big guns!

We met in person, and I loved her. Very direct, which is what works for me. At the end of the session, she asked if I would like to come back. I absolutely did. I asked if she had space in her practice. She told me that she was actually overbooked but would take me on. I asked why. Her response: because of my "level of trauma." Yes, I am still seeing her.

The Gift of Empathy

DOES EXPERIENCING TRAUMA AND GRIEF MAKE YOU more empathetic or less? I found that my mother was not particularly empathetic to other people in times of crisis. She personalized the trauma, worrying that it could happen to her. She was trying so hard to keep herself together and, for her, that meant maintaining distance from other people's tragedies. As if they were contagious.

I was twenty-six years old when Naomi's father passed away from a heart attack at the age of fifty-five. This was my first up-close exposure to the death of someone I knew and cared about. As I walked the short distance between our houses on that freezing cold day in December, having just flown to Montreal from Toronto, I was terrified. What do I say? How do I react to people in the throes of grief?

When Naomi's father died, I assumed that my mother would be part of her mother Roselle's support network. Our parents still lived across the street from each other. But my mother was not there for Roselle. My father was. He would stop by and check in on her. He would escort Roselle to the opera and the symphony.

My mother kept a wide berth. She did not visit. She did not bring meals. I was so disappointed in her behaviour. How can you turn your back on people who are suffering?

It was that experience that taught me how respond to people dealing with grief. You just show up. You be there. And that's what I did. At one point, Naomi and I went for a walk. She wanted to talk about her father. I listened.

Before I left to go back to Toronto a few days later, Roselle pulled me aside and told me to take care of Naomi. I assured her I would. And I did. I picked her up from the airport when she flew back. I went to her apartment every day after work for months.

Naomi was steadfast in her support of me when my parents died. I appointed her my gatekeeper. The only one I would listen to if she saw me going off the rails. At the time, I didn't realize how hard that was on her. To watch someone that you love disintegrating and, despite doing everything you can, being powerless.

And then I understood.

On July 5, 2020, Naomi was at the cottage with her husband Mike, their children, Loren and Adam, and Nick, Loren's fiancé. They were waiting for Mike to return from a quick outing on the lake in his scull boat before heading back to Toronto. Naomi and I happened to be texting each other. She casually mentioned that Mike was missing. I asked her if she was serious. She said she was. The kids went out on the lake to see if they could find him. While they were gone, an Ontario Provincial Police (OPP) boat pulled up to their dock. There had been an accident. Mike had been hit by a jet ski that was going too fast. Mike was hit directly. Not the boat . . . Mike.

The impact sent him flying before he dropped into the lake and disappeared under the water. The OPP explained that there was a recovery mission under way. Not a search and rescue . . . recovery. There were multiple OPP boats and a helicopter involved in the search. We didn't know those details when Michael and I immediately headed to their cottage. We understood that something terrible had happened, but we clung to the hope that although Mike may be seriously injured, perhaps he was able to swim ashore somewhere, and was waiting to be rescued. By the time we arrived at the cottage two and half hours later, we had the full picture. Everyone was in shock. A few hours later, Naomi received a call that Mike had been located. Mike was fifty-eight. Naomi, fifty-six. Loren was supposed to have gotten married the previous weekend, but the wedding had been postponed due to COVID.

It was impossible to believe that Mike was gone. I couldn't process it. And even if there was a way to, I was focused on Naomi and the kids. COVID restrictions were still in place, so the funeral took place at the cemetery and was live streamed. Only twenty people were allowed to attend in person. It was a scorching hot day.

The Shiva also had to be managed. Three of us established the protocol and sent out an email to hundreds of people. People had to sign up for a specific time slot. They could only stay for thirty minutes. They needed to disinfect their hands. No physical contact. No hugging. The Shiva took place in the backyard, so masks were optional. Caroline, a close friend, and I stood near the front of the house with the list of people and their appointment times.

Once the Shiva was over, what lay ahead was the long, snaking road of grief. Like me, Naomi internalizes her pain and has difficulty asking for help. I told the office that I was taking the next month off. Naomi had been my gatekeeper. Now I was hers. I was central command. Friends and family relied on me to provide updates, answer questions, give messages of hope which, of course, I could not do at that point.

What I could do, was be there. To talk about whatever Naomi wanted to talk about. To listen. To bring over her favourite pizza. To be there whenever she wanted me to be and even when she didn't want me to be. One day at her house, she told me, "This is a forever thing." And of course it is. Mike was not at Loren and Nick's wedding. He will never meet his granddaughters; Mikaela, named in his honour, and Rosie, named for Roselle. He wasn't at his son Adam's wedding to Taylor in Italy. There is always a sense of loss clinging to the joy.

If you are lucky enough to have people in your life that you care deeply about, then you have unwittingly been entered into a cosmic ping-pong tournament of grief. The balls kept flying.

Giorgina was a work associate who had become a close friend. We had coffee a few weeks after my parents died. Giorgina is pragmatic and her friendship was deeply comforting. A few years later, while on vacation in Florida with her husband Peter, he suffered a catastrophic stroke and then a brain bleed. He survived, but he had permanent physical and mental impairments. Giorgina is a superhero. She had a big job as a publishing executive and cared for Peter at home for eight years. I am in awe of her. Michael and I would go out with them socially to movies and dinners. Peter was able to navigate in a wheelchair and scooter.

Although his condition was deteriorating, Peter was doing okay, until he fell and suffered a brain injury which he could not recover from.

And the losses kept mounting. My friend Fern and I had known each other since elementary school. Our families had gone on that family mission to Israel together. We drifted after high school but stayed in touch. She got married and moved to Toronto. A serial entrepreneur, she was one of my first clients when I launched OverCat. When my parents died, she came to Montreal for the funeral. I had heard that her husband Pierre was diagnosed with cancer. I didn't reach out. Then a mutual friend told me that it was terminal. I didn't reach out. Then Pierre passed away. I was ashamed that I hadn't been there to support her.

I attended the funeral. While we were seated waiting for it to start, Fern came out from the back room. I think we were all startled to see her, and nobody knew quite what to do. I stood up and walked over to her. I gave her a hug, and she whispered in my ear that she knew I, too, understood profound grief. We began to see each other frequently. We have re-established our friendship and I am so grateful to have her back in my life.

Many addiction counsellors are recovering addicts. Maybe grief is the same. You have to have lived through it to help others navigate theirs.

Deep friendships are not about being there during the good times. They are forged during the bad ones. If I can be preachy for a moment, DO NOT HEAD FOR THE HILLS when the people you love need you. It's not about you. Don't assume that people would rather be left alone. They don't. They want to rebuild their lives, and if you can play any role in that, try to find the strength to do it. You may find that being empathetic to others also helps heal your soul. It has for me.

Addicted to Grief

THE STEADFAST REFUSAL TO LET MY PARENTS ENTER MY REALM of consciousness persisted for fifteen years. The boxes shipped to my house, full of things that I chose to keep when we sold their house, were still taped shut and languishing in the basement. Pictures, silverware, my mother's glass figurines, and the knitting bag that she and Lindsay spent hours using.

I was firmly committed to not examining my life prior to their deaths. If you have ever tried to put an unwilling cat into a carrier, then you will understand. The cat will do anything not to be stuffed in. Limbs splayed across the opening, claws out, hissing.

And then we bought a new house. I was forced to face my pain and go through those boxes. It was the pictures that I dreaded the most. And then something unexpected happened.

There were my parents, looking happy. They were still newlyweds, posing in front of their car in Iowa after a huge snowfall. Cuddling six-week-old me on the balcony of their first apartment in Montreal. But it was one picture in particular that shifted my focus. My mother in a gown, my father in a tuxedo. Looking at each other with so much love. They looked very young. I suspect it must have been taken before I was born.

I finally started writing the book that had been bubbling up inside me for over a decade. I also decided to attend my first Holocaust conference. One that focused on the children of survivors, since so many of the survivors themselves were no longer alive.

Now that I was finally confronting my mother's past, I became curious about other children of survivors. Did their parents' Holocaust experiences dominate their lives as well? Were they more messed up than me? At sixty-one years of age, I was going to brave entering a world of people who were just like me. The conference was taking place in Toronto. It was as if the universe was daring me not to attend.

The conference was an hour's drive away. As I got closer, my anxiety was running rampant. And then I was there, walking through the revolving door into the hotel's atrium, following the signs to registration. The women at the desk were lovely. They complimented me on my outfit. Of course, I had thought that through. My hair was blown out, my makeup perfect. I wore a long black blazer over skinny jeans tucked into butterscotch leather knee-high boots that I just bought. My nails matched the boot colour exactly. Gucci crossover bag firmly in place. If they handed out awards for best dressed at a grief conference, I would have won hands-down.

Right after I registered, I bumped into the mother of a boy my son had played hockey with two decades ago. We looked at each other and realized we knew each other. I didn't know she was the child of survivors. The first thing she said to me was that she had watched my presentation for the Simon Wiesenthal Centre and that she found it powerful. Six months earlier, I had done a virtual speech for the Centre about my family's story.

We walked together to the first meeting, an orientation for "first-timer" attendees. There were three hundred attendees in total from across Canada and the US. One hundred of us were first-timers. I learned that there is a whole lexicon to being the child of a Holocaust survivor. You could be a "2G" second generation, which means that you are a child of a survivor. A "3G," which means you are the grandchild of a survivor. There are even "4G's," the great grandchildren of survivors. I am both a 2G and a 3G. Lindsay is a 3G and a 4G.

The moderator was very good, doing her best to make us feel comfortable and let us know what to expect over the next two and a half days. There were also rules. The conference was a safe space, which meant we did not use other people's names or stories outside of the conference. I have never attended AA meetings, but this protocol seemed to reflect the same ideology. There were other parallels as well.

The conference attendees all seemed to be at different stages in their recovery. A few seemed solidly "sober," living happy lives having come to terms with their trauma. The largest group, of which I would include myself, were "in recovery," still finding our way. And then there were the people who seemed to still be in the throes of their addiction, at high risk of being swallowed up by their unhappiness. But no matter the stage of recovery we were in, ALL of us were still searching. And that search meant we wanted to hear each other's stories. What was your life like growing up? Is your trauma worse than mine? How much does it still affect you? And the holy grail for Holocaust survivors, connections to people who may have known our families, those who could share details with us that we did not know.

After my parents died, I read a lot of biographies about celebrities who were recovering addicts. To me, the experience of surviving trauma and dealing with substance abuse are similar journeys. We have to take our lives one day at a time. Sometimes, one hour at a time. Through a combination of genetics and environment, trauma (like addiction) inhabits the very fibre of our being. We will always be in recovery.

The conference offered breakout sessions, where smaller groups of about forty attendees gathered to discuss topics that were of interest to them. These sessions allowed us to connect one-on-one. Many attendees had two survivor parents, some only one. There appeared to be several different types of households—angry, permissive to the point of negligence, and overprotective. But the undercurrent was always the same: fear. Some survivors told their children to prepare "go" bags, in case they had to evacuate their homes quickly. They lived in the US.

A number of the 2Gs shared that their parents had horrible marriages, married out of circumstance and not affection. They said their parents essentially hated each other. I had not been exposed to any of this. My understanding is that Jack and my grandmother truly loved each other, as did my parents.

Others described basically being ignored and left on their own from a very young age, as early as seven, because both parents were working. These children were also often left in charge of younger siblings.

And then there were the overprotective parents, which was my scenario. So many other 2Gs described not being allowed to swim, or ski, or ride bikes.

But all of us, no matter which type of family category we fell into, felt an obligation to protect the survivor parent or parents. My situation was a bit different because only one of my parents was a survivor, but it does offer a plausible explanation of my father's loyalty to my mother. Once, during a period when my mother was being especially erratic, I asked my father why he didn't leave her. He told me he loved her, and he felt sorry for her.

I learned about Adult Children Syndrome, characterized by the inability to navigate adult decisions and relationships due to the long-term impact of childhood trauma. The term "adult child" was first used in this context by the organization Adult Children of Alcoholics (ACA). While the concept of the adult child was originally developed to explain a personality type of children who were raised by addicts, it is also believed to be valid for the adult children of narcissistic, traumatized, depressed, numbed, workaholic, abusive, and "borderline" or psychotic parents.

I was twenty-one when I attended that therapy session with my mother in Montreal, where the therapist posited that my mother was the child, and I, the adult. Forty years later, I learned it is an actual documented syndrome.

One of the most startling revelations was around separation anxiety, something that had been an ever-present source of conflict between my mother and me since I was a child. I just didn't get it. Wasn't I supposed to grow up and become independent? Wasn't that a sign of successful parenting? And then an attendee spoke about separation in a way that I had never heard it described. In a survivor's mind, separation doesn't mean we left. It means we disappeared, and those are very different things. My mother's father disappeared. So did her grandparents, aunts, uncles, cousins, and childhood friends. Disappearing meant death. So, when I went to sleep-away camp and my mother went bananas, or when she fell apart for three years after I moved to Toronto, she wasn't missing me. She was mourning me.

Every time an attendee mentioned that they were from Poland, I asked what town they were from, but none that I spoke with were from Tomaszów. And then something extraordinary happened. In one of the breakout sessions, we were asked to briefly introduce ourselves. The woman sitting directly behind me, who was the last to speak, said she was born in Feldafing. My head whipped around to look at her. I asked her: "You were born in Feldafing?" She nodded yes.

Lunch was being served after that session, and I asked if I could sit with her. I told her my mother's story, and how my mother had mentioned all the second marriages that took place in Feldafing and the babies that started being born. This woman was one of the first babies to be born in Feldafing. Her family must have known my mother and grandmother! She told me about a book that was written about Feldafing and a Facebook group that exists. Maybe there are pictures and stories about them. I am still wading through those resources.

As the 2Gs shared their stories, it became evident to me that we were in an impossible conundrum. Our survivor parents were miracles. As their children, we knew this. But we also longed to have what we perceived to be "normal" parents. Parents who were not filled with pain and loss and fear and anger. In their haste to rebuild their lives, we, as their children, inherited their bruises. Bruises that never faded. Bruises that hurt when you press on them. Bruises that are not visible to the outside world.

When I started writing this memoir, I was told by the amazing people who were helping me, that you must leave blood on the page, but the book can't be too depressing, or no one will want to read it. I had to end on a hopeful note.

I was also warned that writing this book would take a toll on me psychologically. And I always responded the same way: "I will be fine." This type A girl with a PhD in compartmentalization? No problem. And for a long time, I was.

Then the nightmares started. I had my first "jump scare" dream, the technique used in horror movies to scare the shit out of the audience. I was somewhere dark, and suddenly, a disfigured man jumped up in front of me. My startled response woke our German Shepherd, Twiggy, both of us looking at each other with "what the fuck" expressions.

In the second dream, I was in my kitchen. It was night, and a bedraggled-looking man opened the sliding glass door at the back of the house and casually walked in. I was screaming at him to leave, but he calmly walked over to the counter, picked up a meat cleaver, and started walking toward Cash, my sleeping Bernese Mountain dog. I woke up just as he stood over Cash with the cleaver raised.

There was indeed a psychological price to be paid for writing this book.

Ripping Open the Past

MY MOTHER AND GRANDMOTHER RARELY SPOKE about the Holocaust. The book *Kinderlager,* which was published in 1998, gave me some insight into my mother, but I always felt it barely skimmed the surface—a sanitized version of her experiences.

In 2023, I was perusing the New York Times bestseller list. There was a book called *The Daughter of Auschwitz*. I was surprised to see that all these years later, there was still interest in the subject. I vowed to never read it. That story would mirror my mother's. Why would I want to expose myself to that level of pain?

A few days later, I was in a Toronto airport en route to Lake Louise, Alberta, for a glamorous International Ski Federation press trip for a client. I stopped in a store to stock up on supplies for the flight. There was the book. This time, I noticed that it was the memoir of Tova Friedman, one of the child survivors who had been profiled along with my mother in *Kinderlager*.

I stood paralyzed in front of the book. My mother and grandparents would likely be mentioned in the book. So, I gave in and bought it, but I was too terrified to read it. I skimmed it a bit on the flight. I couldn't sleep that night, so I googled Malcolm Brabant, who co-wrote the book with Tova. In addition to being an author, Malcolm is a Peabody Award-winning journalist for covering conflicts around the world, and the European correspondent for PBS. I decided to message him on social media, explaining who I was and that I would like to connect with him. He responded quickly, agreeing to a Zoom meeting a few days later. I hoped that maybe he would be interested in helping write my book.

I was ecstatic when Malcolm agreed to collaborate. I was finally going to be able to get this book going. We began to meet virtually—Malcolm looked and sounded like a war correspondent from central casting. Bald, sturdily built, with a booming voice. And then, Malcolm sent me a draft of the first chapter. I hated it. It opened with a description of the smoke belching from the chimneys of the crematorium in Auschwitz. This was not the book I wanted to write. I was more focused on the aftermath of trauma. I did a major edit and sent it back to him.

I received a very snarky email in return telling me that he had decided not to work with me on the book. I didn't respond immediately. I was devastated by his rejection. A few days later, I wrote an email acknowledging that I understood and hoped we could stay in touch. He offered to support me where he could.

Over the next two years, while I settled in and finally started writing the book, Malcolm stayed true to his word. He was both supportive and brutally honest. I sent him the book pitch, he hated it. I sent him chapters; he hated those too. Eventually, we found our rhythm and I came to appreciate his tough love approach. I knew he was genuinely trying to help me. He would reach out every few months, asking about my progress and inquiring about publishers and agents I was in touch with.

One day, I mentioned to a family member that I was writing a book. Without saying a word, they went upstairs and returned with a Cerlox-bound notebook. I asked what it was. They said they hadn't read it. They had completely forgotten about it until I mentioned my book.

When I got home, I realized it was the unedited transcripts of my mother's interviews with Milton Nieuwsma for *Kinderlager*. Sixteen years after her death, I was miraculously now in possession of her story in her own words.

I stayed up late into the night pouring over the interviews. I found out that she knew she was out of control and was trying, unsuccessfully, to harness her emotions. She acknowledged that she wrestled with her fears. She would examine them and try to suppress them, but even if she was able to do that for short periods of time, they would get reactivated by various triggers and she would have to battle them again.

She also discussed her relationship with her mother, and her relationship with me, citing them as key sources of conflict in her life. She felt she had outpaced the demons, even achieved brief moments of normalcy and joy, but remained troubled and bore emotional scars.

When she hit a stumbling block, she would try to assess it rationally. My moving to Toronto ripped open the scars. She couldn't bear that I had left her nest. She couldn't get comfortable with the hellos and goodbyes that came with me living in another city. She said that for her, it wasn't possible to heal everything. It was an unattainable goal. She talked about her wounds, her level of anxiety, how her life was a constant battle of trying to rein in her emotions. And mostly failing to do so.

This is one of the central tragedies of our story. Why couldn't she express those things to me? I like to think I would have understood. Maybe then I could have navigated our relationship better than I did. But she didn't share those thoughts with me, she shared them with a stranger.

I got in touch with Milton and asked for permission to use material from the transcripts. He generously agreed. A few months later, he sent me an email letting me know that there was a possibility that *Kinderlager* would be reprinted. He confirmed what I had long suspected, that my mother insisted on a massive rewrite of her section of the book. The result was the detached, unemotional narrative that I always had trouble digesting. For the reprint he went back to his original copy which was more honest and impactful. As he could no longer seek permission from her, he asked me to review it. It was the portrayal that should have been included in the original book, but now there was an addendum, stating that my mother had taken her own life.

In November 2024, I received a WhatsApp message from Malcolm. Would I consider going to Poland to shoot a feature for PBS Newshour? He was interested in retracing my family's Holocaust experiences for a story covering the eightieth anniversary of the liberation of Auschwitz, which was coming up in January.

Malcolm had been pushing me to do a trip to Poland since we first connected. He felt it would be an important part of the book. Up until then, I had resisted. I clawed my way out of the black hole. Why would I risk stumbling back into it? I knew the basics of my mother's and grandparents' story. I had never wanted to know more. Why would I need to? The shadow of the Holocaust was always with me. I didn't need to go to Poland to feel it.

Malcolm, however, was very enthusiastic about doing the trip. He told me it would be the "trip of a lifetime." I told him that I would do it if Lindsay was also part of the story. PBS agreed. Suddenly, I was booking flights and hotels. We were leaving in two weeks. Lindsay and I stocked up on thermal clothing. We would be shooting a lot of the story outside and I didn't want us to freeze.

Naomi was not keen on me doing the trip. She went on a similar voyage with her mother years ago to Belgium, where her mother had been a hidden child. She found the trip and the emotional aftermath difficult.

Naomi also brought up that the trip might be too difficult for Lindsay. She knew first-hand the kind of pain we would be exposing ourselves to. I was so wrapped up in my own misgivings that I had not considered that side of things. When I discussed it with Lindsay, she told me that she had always wanted to do the trip. I suspect that she probably never would have done it because I would have been violently opposed to it. But now I was making it okay.

As the trip got closer, I worried that I would be an emotional disaster, making it more difficult on Lindsay. I discussed my concerns with her promising that I would do my best to hold it together. Her response was interesting. Lindsay has done a great deal of self-examination. She told me that it was important for both of us to feel whatever we felt, and not censor ourselves. She did not want me to hide my emotions from her, nor did she want to hide hers from me. We would support each other wherever the journey took us. My wise daughter.

There was a small part of me that worried we were being catfished as I planned the trip. I had never met Malcolm in person. What if this was some elaborate scheme to bring us to Poland for some reason that I couldn't fathom? There were frequent dispatches on a WhatsApp group outlining our shooting schedule for the week. What if it was all a ruse?

And then we were on a flight to Warsaw. The man sitting across the aisle from me had a terrible cold. He was blowing his nose throughout the eight-and-a-half-hour flight. He was not wearing a mask. Stupidly, neither was I.

I had arranged for a car pick-up from the Warsaw airport. Initially, we couldn't find the driver, but we eventually saw him standing with a sign bearing my name on it. Lindsay and I piled into a huge Mercedes van. The irony was not lost on me. My mother and grandmother left Poland with nothing. Almost eighty years later, my daughter and I were in a luxury car, heading to a luxury hotel, wielding suitcases packed with well-thought-out outfits that balanced warmth and fashion, and were appropriate for being on camera.

By the time we arrived at the hotel, my nose was running like a faucet, and I had developed a hacking cough. Panic! What if I flew all this way and got too sick to shoot? We had a crazy schedule shooting over six days. Luckily, I didn't develop a fever, and my energy level, probably fueled by anxiety, was on high.

Malcolm and Trine, his wife and frequent field producer, were arriving late that night so we arranged to meet up in the morning. Lindsay and I were exhausted. We ordered pizza and ate in bed.

The next morning, we were the first to arrive in the lobby, anxious about what lay ahead. Suddenly, there were Malcolm and Trine. They were real. This was happening.

Malcolm is a brilliant journalist and he'd planned a comprehensive journey for us. First up were the background interviews that would provide the context for our trip.

We both knew that Malcolm would not let us get away with skimming the surface of our story. That he would dig for the emotional impact. But much like going into childbirth, while you can intellectually process what is about to happen, you can't possibly prepare for that level of pain.

Malcolm arranged to film the interviews in a synagogue close to the hotel. As we approached, we could see that it was completely barricaded behind a fence. The only entry point was a side door with a camera trained on it. You had to be buzzed in for access. Police patrolled outside the synagogue. A security office was stationed inside the door.

It was a small two-story building with a soaring ceiling. Malcolm and Trine set up on the second floor, with a view overlooking the chapel. I am used to being around cameras, both as a producer and as a subject, but this was different. I wasn't discussing an event I was planning. I was talking about my family.

We were wearing microphones. The camera followed us everywhere. Malcolm gave us directions on where to stand, where to walk. It was unnerving. Like we were shooting a horror-filled episode of *The Real Housewives* franchise.

I did my first interview, which lasted about thirty minutes. I talked about my family's history during the war and about my parents' death. I talked about how my mother and grandmother would not be happy that Lindsay and I were in Poland. Their whole lives had been dedicated to separating us from this place. Now we had returned to peer under the rocks and examine my family's legacy of trauma and death.

Malcolm asked if he could shoot us watching part of my mother's Shoah tape. I didn't know that he was planning that. Lindsay and I sat next to each other on a bench with the computer on my lap. While I had recently found the courage to sift through our family photos, this was different. Suddenly, there she was. She looked beautiful. I had forgotten how beautiful she was. She was composed and spoke eloquently. It was jarring to see her. I couldn't really process it. As she continued speaking, I became overwhelmed. Malcolm was there to document it all as I fell apart, sobbing on Lindsay's shoulder.

When we were done, we walked over to the remains of the Warsaw ghetto. Maybe there is a plaque commemorating the history of the site, but I didn't see one. There was graffiti on the walls and a thin, frayed rope meant to keep people out. I'm not sure what I was expecting, but it was not that. No reverence for the people had who had staged a valiant uprising. No mention of the people who died there. No recognition of the horrors that had taken place in plain sight of the city's inhabitants. I found it deeply disturbing.

That evening, Malcolm had arranged for a virtual interview with Tony Bernard, a physician who is based in Australia and the author of *The Ghost Tattoo*, which detailed his father's Holocaust experience as a member of the Jewish Police in Tomaszów. The same town where my grandparents had lived. Malcolm had a very specific reason for arranging the interview.

During one of our initial conversations, Malcolm had told me that when he was researching *The Daughter of Auschwitz*, he came across documentation showing that my grandfather had been a member of the Jewish Police in the Tomaszów ghetto.

The Jewish Police were appointed by the Jewish Council, the organizational body who the Nazis assigned to run the ghetto. That was the first time I had heard anything about this. I told Malcolm his information was incorrect. He then sent me a scanned page from a Nazi ledger that showed that my grandfather was being paid to fulfill this position. I still didn't believe him. How could I not know this? It felt impossible that my family had a secret of this magnitude. Malcolm was unwavering.

Following a few technical glitches, there was Tony, at 6 a.m. Australia time, sharing his family's story. But it wasn't just his story. He was convinced that it was mine as well.

The Jewish Council had been ordered by the Nazis to appoint forty-two Jewish Policemen. He said there was a concerted effort to select men who were of good character. Men who would not abuse the authority that had been forced on them. They were responsible for keeping the ghetto's inhabitants compliant. Making sure that they didn't escape. Escorting them to work assignments. Enforcing the deportation process.

The Jewish Police were not immune from being killed. Neither were their families. If orders were not followed by the Council and enforced by the Jewish Police, the Nazis would take it out on them.

In late October and early November of 1942, the selections began to clear out the ghetto. Apparently, if you were a member of the Jewish Police, you were allowed to choose one person to save. My mother and grandmother both made it through the selections. Two percent of the Jews in Tomaszów survived the selections. Just over one percent survived the war. Five little girls, including my mother, were the only children to survive.

Tony was certain that my mother and grandmother had survived only because my grandfather was a member of the Jewish Police. This reinforced my mother's recollection of my grandfather frequently disappearing and reappearing. Was he carrying out official duties?

He also explained that many of the Jewish Police held positions of authority in the labour camps. From Tomaszów, my mother and grandparents were sent to the Starachowice labour camp. I don't know if my grandfather held such a position there.

In June 1944, my mother and grandmother boarded that cattle car destined for Auschwitz. My grandfather boarded the train bound for Dachau. I have been told that there is another possible narrative about how my grandfather died on the train. That there may have been someone else involved in his death. We will never know what actually happened.

It was becoming harder to deny the growing body of evidence about my grandfather. But what did he do and not do? He likely saved his wife and child. Maybe he saved other people as well? Could he have said no to being a member of the Jewish Police? In those circumstances, where Jewish lives were irrelevant and the risks were life and death, did anyone have a choice? Tony had likely wrestled with these same demons. He told me he truly believed that my grandfather taking that job is the reason I exist today. The reason that my children exist. Without my grandfather's position, my family would have almost certainly perished.

It was a lot to process.

Early the next morning, we drove to Tomaszów. We arrived at a low-slung building that housed Tomaszów's historical documents from the war. We were meeting Justyna Biernat, who wrote the book *Children of the Tomaszów Mazowiecki Ghetto*, which was published in 2023.

Justyna and I began conversing two years ago when Malcolm suggested I contact her to try to find out more information about my family. This was our first time meeting in person.

Justyna, now a PhD candidate, grew up in Tomaszów. She became interested in the history of the Jews from that city while doing academic research. She found that there was no definitive recorded history on the topic, and felt compelled to write about it. When I first reached out to her, she and her co-editors were in the final stages of the book. She had been trying to find out more about my family and I was able to provide her with some of the information she was looking for. When the book was published, she asked me to send her a video talking about my family, which was shown at the book launch.

I didn't know what to expect when I met Justyna, but it was not this spunky, chicly dressed woman. We hugged like old friends. I showed her pictures of my family. We spoke Yiddish to each other.

Justyna then put on a pair of gloves and began showing us the documents that pertained to my family. Dates that people arrived in the ghetto, what year they left . . . if they left. Then she brought out the ledger containing the record of the Jewish Council and Jewish Police in Tomaszów. This was the ledger that contained the page that Malcolm had emailed to me. The ledger listed the names of people who were being paid, what amount they were paid, and on which date. My grandfather's name was clearly included on multiple pages of the handwritten, meticulous ledger.

Justyna explained that some members of the Jewish Police were paid higher salaries than others, which meant they were in positions of authority. My grandfather was not one of the higher-paid individuals.

My grandmother had to have known. The Jewish Police wore uniforms. My mother was so young, it is likely she would not have known the significance of her father's clothing, even if she did remember it. The bigger question was, did my mother ever know?

Malcolm was able to shed some light on that. When Malcolm was co-writing *The Daughter of Auschwitz*, he had been in touch with Milton. Milton revealed that he had told my mother about her father's potential role in the Jewish Police. This was apparently when she learned about it.

Maybe that's why she went into such a decline when the book came out and refused to participate in the press? She wanted to keep her father's secret.

I will never know if she discussed it with my grandmother. Clearly, my grandmother had kept this information hidden from my mother for all those years.

And the inevitable question. How do *I* feel about this information? My grandfather was always a ghost to me. A sepia-toned picture of a handsome man in a fedora. Maybe my mother's and grandmother's survival was not the miracle I thought it was, but the direct result of a man willing to go to great lengths to save his family. Did other Jews hold him responsible for the death of their loved ones? Did my family's survival come on the backs of others? Would I have done any differently in his position?

I wrestled with including this information in my book. I was revealing an eighty-year-old secret. I spoke to a few people about this dilemma. Michael felt that we didn't necessarily know the whole story and that I shouldn't include it. Others felt that if I was confronting my family history, then it should be included. Ultimately, I agreed. It underscores the secrets that were passed down through the generations of my family. And the catastrophic consequences.

The next filming location was St. Wenceslas Church, originally located on Wajtsznosc Street. The place where the 1942 selections had taken place. It had been moved to a different location to make room for a bigger, more modern church, but the original small wooden church had been preserved. When we arrived, I stood on the road. I didn't even want to walk on the grass leading up to it. Lindsay had the same visceral reaction. This house of worship symbolized death. Lindsay said she could feel the evil there. We kept our distance and were relieved when we left.

Our next location was the tenement house in the ghetto, where my family had been forced to live. The building is still standing and Justyna knew a lot about my family's history there. They occupied three one-bedroom flats (two on the main floor and one on the second floor). There were approximately ten family members in each one-bedroom flat. My mother and her parents lived in a second-floor flat.

I paused in the main doorway entrance. For a moment, I toyed with the idea of refusing to enter, but I knew that wasn't an option. I had agreed to do this and so, like the people pleaser that I am, I stepped inside.

The building was still in its original state, but it was under renovation. I don't know if it had been occupied since the war. It was just another building in a neighbourhood. Nothing to betray the suffering that had taken place within its walls.

There was plywood and dust everywhere. The doors to the units on the main floor were open, so we wandered in. They appeared to be unchanged since my family members lived there. The ceilings were low, the flat was tiny, a tall and ancient heating unit stood in the corner of the main room.

From my privileged, willfully ignorant life in Toronto, I could avoid facing the truth. It was easy to cling to the few historical details I knew. Who died. Who lived. I kept them as just facts, somewhat distant from me and my reality. But now, I was confronted with how they lived as their futures became increasingly perilous.

We walked upstairs to the flat on the second floor. There was plastic over the door. We tried to open it, but this unit, number 9, was locked. We knocked on the door but expected no response. We were wrong. A young, pretty, blonde woman opened the door. We all stared at each other for a moment in shock. We explained who we were and why we were there.

The young woman let us enter the apartment. Her name was Emily, and she was a twenty-four-year-old radio announcer who lived there with her parents. Her family had built the building before the war but were forced to leave when the Nazis appropriated it.

Unlike the rest of the building, this flat was completely renovated. It turns out that if we had been there a few weeks earlier, it would have still been in its original state. Emily and her family had just moved in. We stood in the cramped entrance. I saw a black-and-white kitchen floor and a shiny Formica counter. Trine asked if we could film in the unit. Emily called her parents to ask them, but they would not give us permission, so we left to shoot outside the building.

Emily was fascinated by us. She came outside to talk. She knew very little about the Jewish history of the building and was curious. Email addresses and phone numbers were exchanged. My head was spinning. I was having trouble breathing. Emily was very sweet, but I didn't want to make small talk when all I could picture was the horrid living conditions and constant state of fear that my family endured in that building. Lindsay and I did our interviews, but I have no idea what I said. I felt like I was barely coherent.

We were finished shooting for the day, so Justyna suggested a nearby restaurant where we could have lunch. The smell of food when we walked in made me nauseous. I knew I wouldn't be able to swallow anything. I didn't want to draw attention to myself, so I ordered a coffee and mashed potatoes, explaining I wasn't hungry. The potatoes were dry, and I thought I would choke on them, so I sat quietly while the animated meal took place around me. I could not wait to get back to the hotel.

Auschwitz was the last location to be filmed. Malcolm had allocated two days for it. Since it gets dark early in Poland in the winter, around 3:30 p.m., exterior shots have to be done first while there is still daylight. The plan was to take a fast train to Krakow early the next morning and then rent a car for the one-hour drive to Auschwitz.

We met in the hotel lobby at 7 a.m. and took the Mercedes van to the train station. We were booked in the VIP car and waited at the end of the platform, where Malcolm believed it would stop. As soon as the train pulled into the station, Malcolm realized we were at the wrong end of the very long platform.

I had two heavy suitcases. In a panic, Malcolm grabbed his suitcase and one of mine. Thankfully . . . I could never have run with both of mine. Luckily, everyone else only had one suitcase. We raced down the platform with Lindsay and Trine trailing behind us. If we missed this train, we would lose the shooting day. My lungs were burning. The train doors closed a few times before we reached our car, but they opened again. By the time we got our luggage onto the car, we were all sweating and panting.

I was racing to make a train so we could get to Auschwitz. The world was upside down.

When we arrived in Krakow two hours later, Lindsay and I took an Uber to our hotel in the city's Old Town to drop off our bags. I booked us into a boutique hotel that was charming. I thought it would be good for us to stay somewhere that was less institutional-feeling than a big hotel chain. We checked in to our room, and then Malcolm and Trine picked us up in a rental car for the one-hour drive to Auschwitz.

How do you mentally prepare yourself for a trip to that place? You can't. For some reason, I had brought with me a pin that belonged to my mother. It was a gold and pearl starburst that I remember her wearing often. I placed it over my heart, underneath my jacket. I wanted to have something of hers with me when we went to the camp.

We followed the signs to *Oświęcim* ("Auschwitz" in Polish). Once we entered the town, my level of dread and anxiety continued to rise. A few miles outside of the camp is a cluster of North American fast-food restaurants. People live here, work here, eat junk food here. They build houses so close to the camp that the barracks and barbed-wire fences are clearly visible from their front yards.

Malcolm and I had decided to shoot the story in early December for several reasons. I wanted to make sure that he had enough time to get the story edited so that it could air before January 27, the actual day of the liberation. I was also worried that the later we went, the colder it would be. Malcolm also knew from experience, having covered the seventy-fifth anniversary of the liberation, that the camp would be overrun with reporters and that a giant tented structure would be erected for the ceremonies, which would block sight lines. Malcolm had been assured that the building of the tent would begin a few days after our interview, but as we drove up, we could see that the tent was already being built. Malcolm was upset because this meant access to the train station was blocked and he wanted to film there. I had wanted to see it too. It left such a strong impression on my mother.

The camp, which is designated a museum, had assigned a curator named Mirek to help us. We met him in the parking lot. He was Polish and lived nearby. He was not Jewish, but he had been with the museum for twenty-six years. He was one of the kindest people I have ever met. Before we entered a building that led into the camp, Malcolm offhandedly mentioned that Mirek said it was very busy today. Busy?

The camp was divided into two sections. Auschwitz I, which was smaller, had been a Polish military base before the Nazis commandeered it. That was where we were shooting on the first day. Auschwitz II, also known as Auschwitz-Birkenau, was much larger and would be our location on the second day.

We passed though an ugly building, and suddenly, we were in Auschwitz I. I was terrified. I grabbed Lindsay's hand. The first thing you see when you enter is the famous *"Arbeit Macht Frei"* gate. "Work Sets You Free." A supposedly inspirational message to the camp's prisoners. I'd seen images of it, but it was much smaller than I imagined—only about 12 feet in length.

What I didn't expect was the hundreds of people walking the grounds. Somehow, I had pictured us as the only ones there. I had no idea that it was such an attraction for people. I reacted very negatively to this. Who were all these "trauma tourists" and why were they here? Lindsay felt differently. She thought it was important for as many people as possible to bear witness to this place. Maybe she is right. But I could not overcome my feelings.

The crowds made it challenging for Malcolm to shoot. He wanted a shot of Lindsay and I walking through the gate, but he didn't want other people in the shot. When there was a break in the crowd, I grabbed Lindsay's hand again and we walked through. Malcolm wanted to shoot from a few different angles, but we kept having to stop to avoid the crowds.

As Lindsay and I stood off to the side, a young woman who looked to be in her early twenties, wearing fuzzy earmuffs with bunny ears, handed her friend her phone and posed smiling in front of the gate. I was dumbfounded. To her, Auschwitz was Instagram-worthy.

There is one gas chamber and crematorium still standing in Auschwitz I. It is much smaller than the ones the Nazis blew up in Auschwitz-Birkenau before they fled.

Malcolm wanted Lindsay and me to film an interview in the gas chamber area, but it was so crowded it seemed unlikely. Then, suddenly, the area seemed to clear out. There were no people, and you could have heard a pin drop. We were able to do the interviews, which took about ten minutes. When we were finished, I looked behind me. There were literally hundreds of people being held back at the entrance to the gas chamber. Mirek and Trine had stopped the crowd from entering the room. They were told that family members of survivors were in the space and asked to wait. I had no idea they were there. It was shocking to see them staring at us in total silence.

We moved to the area where the crematorium was. The crowds had now been allowed to come in, so Lindsay and I waited our turn to move to the front. When we reached it, I completely broke down. It didn't matter that there were people watching me sob. The horror was just too much for me. Lindsay and I exited the building.

Malcolm wanted to interview us again. I still had tears streaming down my face. He asked me what I was thinking about. I told him it was the children. Children, who could have been my mother, shovelled into the crematorium and burned to ash.

It took me a while to regain my composure. It was Mirek who was able to calm me down. He asked me about my family's story. He just kept repeating that he could not believe that my mother survived. At this point, Malcolm was back filming inside the crematorium, but because I was mic'd, he could hear our conversation. He came running out of the building, grabbed Lindsay's mic, and put it on Mirek. This was not part of the original plan, but he felt our conversation was meaningful enough to record.

We were losing daylight and Malcolm had another shot he wanted to capture, the wall where the Nazis lined people up to shoot them. It was about 10 feet long and 8 feet high and sat at the end of a row of barracks. You could see bullet holes in the brick. This was a place of no mercy. If you were marched in front of the wall, you were killed.

The barracks themselves had been well preserved. Haunting black-and-white photographs hung on the wall. One of the pictures depicted about eight children in prisoner uniforms. One of them looked just like my mother. Lindsay noticed it, too. We stood in front of it, deliberating whether it was her or not. For some reason, I wanted it to be. I'm not sure why, but I was overwhelmed by the possibility that this young girl could be my mother. Mirek was able to track down the names and it turned out to not be her.

On the opposite wall were individual pictures of children, mostly teenagers. The fear in their eyes was palpable. I was drawn to a picture of a beautiful girl. She did not survive.

When I turned around, there was a photo I had somehow missed. Three little boys, they looked to be around ten years old, with their arms around each other, smiling for the camera. They were completely emaciated. It did not even seem possible that they could be alive. Or that they were smiling. These were the pictures I could not bear. I told Lindsay that I had to leave, and I stepped outside. She came with me.

In several interviews, Malcolm asked me if I was "happy" that I had come on the trip. I think what he was trying to get at was my emotions about the journey. I couldn't process a response. I told him I wasn't prepared to answer that yet.

The last barracks we visited had a display of eyeglass frames behind a glass wall. Thousand of them, maybe tens of thousands of them. Twisted, black metal that was fused together. If you didn't know the origin of these glasses, you might think they were an interesting sculpture, rather than a reminder that the people who wore them were exterminated.

I was grateful when Malcolm said we were done for the day. On the drive back to the hotel, Malcolm and Trine were discussing that day's footage. Lindsay was quiet. I closed my eyes and fell asleep.

Once we got back, Lindsay and I decided to explore Old Town and find somewhere to have dinner. The streets and restaurants were packed, but we found a lovely little place and had pizza. And wine. After dinner, we walked the main street back to our hotel. There were dozens of cute little shops. Lindsay stopped in front of one that had a beautiful display of ceramic hot air balloon

Christmas ornaments. Off to the side, she noticed a ceramic sunflower. My mother's favourite flower. It felt like a sign.

While in Krakow, Malcolm and Trine were shooting another story about a project that was preserving the shoes from Auschwitz. They decided it would be a good idea to give Lindsay and I the day off. It was also Friday the thirteenth, and I think Malcolm believed that somehow made it worse. I was actually hoping to get everything over with. It turns out Malcolm was right that we needed a break. We slept until 3 p.m. in the afternoon. We were still exhausted but decided that we should get up.

We eventually left the hotel. Because I had requested that Mirek accompany us again when we returned to Auschwitz on Saturday, I wanted to get him a bottle of scotch to thank him. There was a liquor store about a mile away from the hotel, so we walked the winding streets looking for it. We came upon a synagogue, which was also fenced off. There was a map of several other synagogues in the area and a sign that said Krakow was dedicated to rebuilding its Jewish community.

Lindsay and I discussed our first day at Auschwitz. I felt that the worst was behind me, but Lindsay was dreading the next day when we would see where my mother and grandmother were imprisoned.

We were hungry but couldn't stand the crowded restaurants, so we ordered McDonalds and ate in bed. We watched the Hugh Grant movie *Heretic*. As if we weren't already experiencing enough horror.

Early the next morning, Lindsay and I picked up coffee and food for the four of us at a little café across from the hotel. Then back we went to Auschwitz. Following the signs again, passing the fast-food restaurants. We parked the car and began the long walk into Auschwitz-Birkenau. It is much larger than Auschwitz I. I had been warned about this by friends who had visited Auschwitz—to be prepared for the sheer size of it. But even armed with that information, it was still overwhelming. The one upside was that even though it also had a lot of visitors, it was so big that we didn't have to interact with anybody.

One of first things you notice is the train tracks. The tracks my mother had referenced, that went on and on into the distance. Malcolm asked Lindsay and I to walk alongside the tracks. There was one cattle car on the tracks but it was behind a fence so we couldn't access it. I felt numb. I glanced over at Lindsay; she looked morose.

Malcolm was filming the surroundings, so Lindsay and I walked ahead. There, on the tracks, was a single red rose covered in frost. It must have been put there recently, because it was not withered or brown. Perhaps the person who left it there was honouring the people who had perished.

We walked over to the crematoriums. While part of the structures had been destroyed, you could still see the remains of the tunnels where the prisoners were marched underground to their deaths. Mirek stood with us. He said this was the worst place on earth.

My mother, at age eight, had been led into one of these underground tunnels in the last months of the camp's existence. She and the other children were told to disrobe. They waited. Nothing happened. Eventually they were brought back to the Kinderlager barracks. I was standing next to where that had happened eighty years ago. It was impossible not to visualize the horror.

I asked Mirek what he thought could have happened. He had a few theories. There may have been a gas shortage or a technical glitch. It could have been when the 175 Jewish men who were tasked with running the crematoriums abandoned their posts and fled. They were all shot. In my mind, that is the scenario that made the most sense. They knew they would be killed but they would not be responsible for the death of any more children.

I had known this story about my mother's brush with death for a long time, but somehow, ridiculously, the impact of it had been lost on me.

In my interview, standing in front of the rubble of the crematorium, Malcolm asked how it felt to know that my daughter and I should not exist. I had never thought of it in those terms. By almost any measure, we should not be standing here. In this terrible place, Lindsay and I were given a future.

Malcolm asked again whether I was happy that I did the trip. I asked him to rephrase it, as that was a question I couldn't answer. Instead, he asked if I regretted it. The answer was no, but I knew I would be haunted by what I saw. And that I never wanted to come here again.

As a child, I obviously could not have understood my mother's grief and pain, but as an adult . . . had I protected myself at her expense? I had never had to physically confront the horrors of her childhood. Knowing about it and seeing it in real life are two very different things.

As we continued our tour, I became obsessed with the numbers.

Approximately 1.3 million people were sent to Auschwitz.

Around 232,000 were under the age of eighteen.

A total of 1.1 million were killed.

On January 27, 1945, seven thousand people were liberated from Auschwitz.

If the ratio of adults to children holds true—and I doubt it does, because children were less likely to survive—then that would mean 1200 out of 232,000 children were liberated. My mother had a 0.5 per cent chance of surviving. How can you possibly process or make sense of that? My mother, Lindsay, me—*we were the girls who should not be.*

There was a headstone commemorating the dead near one of the crematoriums. Malcolm asked if Lindsay or I wanted to put stones on it. This is a Jewish tradition. When you visit a cemetery, you place a rock on the headstone. Lindsay didn't want to go anywhere near it, but I did. Malcolm helped me find two stones. A larger one and a smaller one. One for my grandmother and one for my mother. It's true, they were not killed at Auschwitz, but they lost so much. Part of them never left here.

Lindsay wanted to visit the barracks where my mother and grandmother were assigned to. Seeing that was what she was most afraid of. We tried to identify the Kinderlager barracks and the infirmary where my grandmother had gone to retrieve my mother and hide them instead of joining the Death March, but we couldn't be sure.

The barracks that we did go into was outfitted with rows of makeshift wooden beds built on top of each other. The barracks were designed to hold two hundred people, but in fact, up to nine hundred were crammed in. Ten people had been assigned to one bunk that was designed for two or three. Lindsay was silent as we walked through.

And then it was over. Malcolm had filmed everything he needed to. We said goodbye to Mirek and gave him the bottle of scotch. Lindsay and I each hugged him. Then he hugged me one more time. We left Auschwitz.

Malcolm and Trine were flying back to the UK that night. We said our goodbyes in front of our hotel. These people who we had met in person only seven days ago were now an indelible part of our lives.

Lindsay and I walked back to the shop that sold the ceramic sunflowers. I bought one for each of us.

Our flight was at 6 a.m. the next morning. We were up at 2 a.m. and left the hotel at 3 a.m. I couldn't sleep on the flight. It was a long trip back. Two hours to Frankfurt, a four-hour layover, and then an eight-hour flight to Toronto. I had been getting progressively sicker throughout the trip. By the time I got home, I had a sinus infection, walking pneumonia, and COVID. I stayed in bed for a week, physically and psychologically exhausted.

I was having a hard time reintegrating. I didn't want to see people. I didn't want to go out and do things. Naomi was right. The trip had taken a toll. I felt like I was somehow morphing into my mother, hiding away from the world in my bedroom. Slowly, I started returning to my normal life. Or my new normal life. The one that now carries the memories of a place I never wanted to confront.

Lindsay told me that right after we returned, she got two sunflower tattoos on her back. A few months later, she had barbed-wire hearts tattooed on each knee. I think that image captures our family history perfectly.

Are You Okay Now?

THAT'S THE GOAL, RIGHT? TO BE OKAY? To emerge from the chrysalis of trauma and grief and become a butterfly. But what if that isn't possible? How do you learn to live with it and, more importantly, how do you break the cycle for your children?

Are you okay now? That question has been lobbed at me so many times since my parents died. A year after their deaths, when my Uncle Max asked me. Five years later, at my high school reunion. And most recently by Malcolm, when we were in Poland. I think being okay, like many things, is on a spectrum. The truth is, I am . . . but also, I am not.

My mother, who had always been in search of answers through books, had a copy of *I'm OK—You're OK*, by Thomas Anthony Harris, beside her bed for years. The bright yellow cover was an ongoing reminder that some of us need to be instructed on how to be okay.

It has been very difficult spending time with my parents again. People ask me if writing the book has been cathartic. It has not.

Mostly, it underscores everything I have lost and reinforced just how doomed my mother likely was. I truly never appreciated or understood the depth of her pain. She was a miracle, and I failed to see it.

My path and my mother's were very different. But her path is part of my journey. I am working on learning to be more grateful for everything I have. For what has been given to me and for what I have earned. I think closure is a fairy tale. Some things are just too big to fully assimilate. I accept that I will only ever be partially okay.

A few years ago, I was flipping through the *New York Times* and noticed an ad from jewellery designer Monica Rich Kosann for a dog tag called the "Dorothy" medallion. It has the words "you had the power all along my dear" engraved on it. These were the words Glinda the Good Witch bestowed upon Dorothy in *The Wizard of Oz* when she was trying to find her way home. Back to her family. Back to a safe space. I bought it for Lindsay.

My grandmother had no power over what happened to her as a young woman, but she did have the strength to build a new life. My mother tried her best to do the same. Her family was the single most important thing in the world to her, and to a great degree, she succeeded.

I was determined to build that safe space, too. To distance myself and my family from the turmoil I grew up with. As much as we want to protect our children, there are so many things that are out of our control. Lindsay has been able to assimilate the strengths and weaknesses of the three generations of women before her. So yes, she did have the power all along.

When I was at summer camp at age sixteen, a boy in my unit dedicated the song "You Can't Always Get What You Want" to me at a Saturday night dance. I was deeply offended at the indictment. I look at it differently now. I realize he was right. It's shocking to me that even at sixteen, I gave off the vibe that I always wanted more. That what I had was never enough. For better or worse, I understand it is my mantra, and it has served me well. I wanted a husband, children, a career, a nice house. I achieved that.

The follow-up line in the chorus of the song is, "But if you try sometimes, you get what you need." Before I even knew what it meant to want, I didn't get what I needed from my mother. Safe harbour, unconditional love, self-confidence. I did get those things from my father, but as with everything in my life, my mother's shadow loomed larger.

It is up to me to strike that balance. Can I fully appreciate everything I have? Did I give Lindsay what she needed? Did I make her journey more difficult? Was I there when she needed me? I still don't know, and I'm not sure I ever will. Just like I'm not sure I will ever be "okay." But maybe, not knowing and not being okay . . . is okay.

Lindsay and I have started taking ballet classes together. Next up, jazz classes. I've already ordered a high-cut leg leotard in neon pink. Fuck it.

My mom and me, six weeks old.

Acknowledgements

Rebecca Eckler and Chloe Robinson from RE:BOOKS, for taking a leap of faith, holding my hand, and believing in me.

My editor Deanna McFadden, who was both terrifying and invaluable.

My publicists Chris Reed and Sasha Stoltz, with gratitude and respect.

The Wilders audio crew, Jody Colero, Asha Dillion, Aidan Cade Goldsmith, Des Da Silva, and Anthony Yordanov.

The proprietors of the first puzzle pieces that helped bring this book to life, Julie Sutherland, Kate Cassaday, and Katrina Onstad.

Malcolm Brabant, journalist extraordinaire who forced me to confront my demons, and to his wife, Trine Villemann, for your unwavering support and kindness.

Deborah McNamara, for not abandoning me when I was a sleep-deprived, impossible boss, and thirty-two years later, for keeping the book from going off the rails.

Naomi Abramowitz Cohen, my soul sister, then, now, forever.

Charlotte Zigler, Sandi Rudin Goodman, Ruthie Rudin, for shining a light in the dark.

In memory of Sheila and Victor Goldbloom, Max Palayew, Ruthie and Marvin Goldsmith, Raymond Rudin, and Mike Cohen.

Eunice Palayew, for your candour, love, and support. You are the bond that keeps the past tethered to the present.

Judy and Mark Bercuvitz, for understanding my seventeen years of silence and loving me in absentia.

Francy, Militie, and the Dines boys, for some of the happiest memories of my childhood and for welcoming me back so many years later.

The Bialik High School gang, Lisa Saltzman, Sharon Cape, Lissa Cohen Shorr, Liane Rashkovan Eliesen, Faygie Bercovitch, and Joan Tucker.

To Laurie Stein, Debbie Siemiatycki, and Gilla Geiger, for the adventures in our youth when we were blissfully unaware of what lay ahead, and for the love and support when we found out.

The Overkittens who rode the bucking bronco of PR with me—Valerie Ackerman, Cristina Allsop, Niside Aloi, Caleigh Randev Anthony, Katherine Clark, Sarah Daniel, Gillian DiCesare, Rachel Evans, Miju Kim, Christine Patterson Landers, Emily MacCulloch, Simona Newton, Sara Piets, Thalia Policicchio, Chelsea Brooks Smith, and Mirissa Valenti.

To Aliki Mahshy for providing me with career opportunities beyond my wildest dreams and riding the wave together for nineteen wonderful years.

Brad Romoff and Rosemary Clark, for your love and friendship.

My Cheerleaders, Amanda Brugel, Sara Waisglass, Giorgina Bigioni, Fern Gordon, Romina DiPasquale, Caroline Freedman, Vida Schultz, Candy Signorini, Brandi Leifso, and Lili Shalev Shawn.

Karen Sickle Delfin, always in my heart.

Emily Haines and Metric, for the song "Help I'm Alive," the soundtrack of my sorrow.

For those very important people in my life who prefer to remain anonymous, you are greatly loved.

Songs by amazing Canadian recording artists played on repeat in my life:

Like a Lover like a Song (1976) – April Wine

White Hot (1979) – Red Rider

Worlds Away (1982) – Strange Advance

Lovers in a Dangerous Time (1984) – Bruce Cockburn

Teenland (1987) – Northern Pikes

Bleed a Little While Tonight (1991) – Lowest of the Low

Lost Together (1992) – Blue Rodeo

It Falls Apart (1993) – The Odds

Brand New Low (2001) – Treble Charger

Hands Clean (2002) -Alanis Morissette

Tired of Waiting (2003) – The Trews

Into the Fire (2006) – Sarah McLachlan

Surrender (2006) – Billy Talent

Help I'm Alive (2008) – Metric

Brand New Bitch (2011) – Anjulie

About the Author

Audrey Hyams Romoff is president of OverCat, a highly respected communications agency specializing in luxury clients. She is an adequate wife, fiercely devoted mother, and over-the-top animal lover. Audrey expertly manages a complex, multifaceted existence wearing a fabulous array of designer outfits. She holds a PhD in compartmentalization and excels at creating the illusion of living a perfectly manicured life.

Website: www.audreyhyamsromoff.com

Instagram: @audreyhyamsromoff

Facebook: @AudreyHyamsRomoff

LinkedIn: Audrey Hyams Romoff

TikTok: @AudreyHyamsRomoff

Made in the USA
Coppell, TX
25 March 2026